AN INTRODUCTION
TO MEDIEVAL
PHILOSOPHY

AN INTRODUCTION
TO MEDIEVAL
PHILOSOPHY

C. F. J. Martin

EDINBURGH UNIVERSITY PRESS

Edinburgh University Press Ltd
22 George Square, Edinburgh

Typeset in Linotype Sabon by
Hewer Text Composition Services,
Edinburgh, and
printed and bound in Great Britain

A CIP record for this book is
available from the British Library

ISBN 0 7486 0790 0

Contents

Preface

I had a great deal of encouragement and help in the early stages of writing this book from my friend and colleague at the University of Glasgow, Professor A. Broadie. I also found extremely helpful the comments of the two anonymous referees to whom Edinburgh University Press sent an earlier draft and those of my copy-editor, Anne Kelleher. My thanks, and those of the reader, are owed to all these three. Any mistakes which remain are my fault, not theirs.

I am also in the debt of the University of Navarre for providing me with a congenial atmosphere in which to work on revising the first draft.

My understanding of the Middle Ages owes an immense amount to Prof. Geach and Prof. Anscombe; also to Prof. Alasdair Macintyre, particularly obviously in chapters 2 and 5. I have tried to avoid garbling or merely parroting his thought, but if I have failed I apologise. Some of the material of chapter 2 appeared in *The Past and the Present: Problems of Understanding* (Grandpont Papers no. 1, Oxford 1993; ed. A.J. Hegarty). I am grateful for permission to re-use this here.

When I was in the last stages of preparing the manuscript for publication, my dearly loved father fell ill and died. I dedicate this book to his memory, though it is not worthy of him. I like to think that parts of it at least might have interested or amused him.

Christopher Martin

1
WHAT IS THIS BOOK?

This book is entitled *An Introduction to Medieval Philosophy*. It is intended as an introduction to, and an overview of, this subject, on which far too little study has been done, and far too little written. I have two sets of readers primarily in mind: firstly, those who are studying or are principally interested in some other facet of medieval life, perhaps literature or history. Such readers should realise that in this book they will mostly find themes which even nowadays could be called 'philosophical': there will be little about the theological, scientific and imaginative background of the period. Space demands this: and in any case, there already exist guides to these other aspects of medieval thought.

It should be stressed, though, that in many ways these other aspects are much more important. It is possible to achieve a good grasp of medieval history and literature without needing much more information about medieval philosophy than that which is provided by the notes of a good text and commentary. On the other hand, it is scarcely possible to read a page without being brought up against some basic theological or scientific concept with which it is vital to be familiar.

However, those who do want to know more about medieval philosophy as such should be given the opportunity: and this book is here to provide it. The information gleaned from notes and commentaries is piecemeal: there is little or no chance of gaining from them an understanding of what medieval philosophy as a whole meant to those who wrote it and read it. It is not enough for readers to have the term 'accident' explained in a footnote to Chaucer, or the term 'law' commented on in an appendix to Dante: these concepts can only be understood in their context. Above all, without some kind of an introduction of the kind provided by this book, readers of medieval works may not notice when they are up against a philosophical concept, and so may not seek even the piecemeal information provided by a commentary. For these readers I hope to supply a general introduction which will help them to notice medieval philosophical ideas wherever they occur, and to explain the basic concepts in the context in which they were worked out. I shall not be giving detailed information about the views of all or even most of those who wrote philosophy in the Middle Ages.

The other group of readers I have in mind are students of philosophy. It is important for them to understand that medieval philosophy is a different kind of activity from that which is called philosophy today. In my opinion it is a much more interesting one. It is hoped that an account of what medieval people thought they were doing when they did philosophy, and how they did it, will be valuable to them.

In the first three sections I intend to, as it were, give an introduction to the introduction: to explain what the subject is and what special difficulties it presents. This means that firstly three questions must be faced: what is philosophy?, what are the Middle Ages?, and what is an introduction?

1.1 WHAT IS PHILOSOPHY?

This is a question that causes problems to staff in philosophy departments when it is asked by outsiders. It is amusing to see how difficult we find it to answer: though it is the sort of question in which philosophers profess to be experts. Here the question need not cause us too much embarrassment: for our purposes, it can be answered quite simply by saying that what most people nowadays understand by 'philosophy' is the discussion, in the approved manner, of the sort of questions that philosophers are interested in. And we know what those questions are: questions to do with knowledge and meaning, to do with ethics and action, and (sometimes) to do with wider and deeper questions such as 'is there a God?' or 'what is time?'.

It may seem to some that this way of answering the question is trivial and circular: but those who feel this should try their hand at producing another answer which is as accurate, before they protest. It is true that this answer leaves quite a lot to be desired. What is principally needed to complete it is a discussion of why it is that all these and only these questions should be of interest to this curious class of people. From the standpoint of history it is possible to give an answer to this supplementary question quite easily.

These typically 'philosophical' questions are the remaining fragments of what was once a much larger and imposing structure: a structure, which, nevertheless, was never completed. The structure was that of the modern ideal of philosophy: the ideal that was put forward by Descartes. His project was that of producing a system of knowledge that would start from self-evident principles – principles that were evident to all rational beings – and embrace everything that could be known by the power of human reason about the world, and crucially about God. It was, then, a vast and comprehensive structure including what we now call natural theology, mathematics, physics, chemistry, biology, psychology, sociology, the theory of history, ethics, the theory of politics, and the theory of art.

This single unified structure does not exist: it never did exist, except as a project that was never to be achieved. What we mean by 'philosophy' today is a collection of fragments of that structure. It is what is left of the structure after all the parts which are interesting to most people have been separated from it and made independent structures on their own: after the sciences have developed new methods, techniques and attitudes and asserted their autonomy.

A serious question, which should worry philosophers, is whether the fragments that remain within their field of study are a thing of value or not? Is 'philosophy' still, as it ought to be if the ideal of Descartes was correct, a framework into which the other different parts of knowledge can be fitted, to form a unified system, or at least the scaffolding or plan with which the structure can be erected? Or is it just a ruin, consisting of a few odd fragments of varying structural importance which happen to have been left on site, after everything that looks as if it might be useful has been carried away to build other structures?

I do not propose to debate this question: I incline to the view that contemporary philosophy is a ruin. But the reader need not share this opinion to come to realise the immense difference there is between what we understand as 'philosophy' – or 'pure philosophy' – and what medieval people would have understood by the word. To bring the reader to realise this is the basic aim of this book.

Our 'philosophy', then, is arguably the ruin of a structure that was never completed. That structure was first planned out after the medieval period: the only continuity there is between medieval philosophy and ours is coincidental. We have to think of the following picture. Medieval thinkers were involved in building a structure of a certain kind – a cathedral, perhaps, would be a suitable analogy. The analogy is particularly apt in that cathedrals, like medieval philosophy, are seldom the product of one overall plan carried out in one project: they are usually things that develop over the generations. The cathedral was demolished and a single set of unified plans drawn up for building another completely different building on its site. Perhaps a museum, a storehouse of all that can be rationally known, suitably arranged, would be a fitting analogy. The museum was never completed: instead, the masons started carrying away the stones of the parts of the building they were working on and using them in buildings they were constructing elsewhere, as self-contained structures, according to their own plans. What we call 'philosophy' is the ruin of the unfinished museum, in which some can still see a valuable framework that the other buildings could be fitted into, while others can see only ruinous fragments. It is no surprise that philosophers, in general, take the view that philosophy still provides a valuable framework which could relate the many disparate buildings of the other parts of knowledge together, while those involved in other parts of knowledge – the masons who carried away the stones for their own buildings, in our analogy – tend to regard philosophy as a valueless ruin.

It may happen – it does happen – that parts of the still-standing ruinous museum which we call philosophy occupy more or less the same place as parts of the disappeared cathedral: it may even happen that the intended function of these fragments corresponds to the function of the matching parts of the cathedral. The still-standing doorways of the museum may be where the doorways of the cathedral were, and so on. But this does not mean that we can read the plans and discussions of the medieval architects that refer to the doorways and take them to be referring to the doorways that we see before us.

In the same way, we cannot – or should not – read medieval philosophers as if they were contributing to the same debates that modern philosophers are involved in. We should not read Anselm's so-called 'Ontological Argument' for the existence of God as if it were a rival version of Descartes's Ontological Argument. Anselm aims to show that even the foolish atheist has in his mind concepts which should be enough to persuade him that there is a God: Descartes attempts to give a strict logical demonstration that God exists in virtue of the very meaning of the word 'God'. The arguments are similar, but they form parts of very different projects.

The reason why we and medieval thinkers are involved in different projects lies in the revolution which Descartes himself brought about. There were already, before his time, signs of decay in the medieval structure of thought: increasing fragmentation and specialisation was a particularly important one. Moreover, the Renaissance humanists had come to despise the inelegance of that structure. Nevertheless, there are good reasons to put Descartes at the start of modern philosophy.

Descartes became convinced that the vast, cathedral-like structure of medieval philosophy was not just decaying but already falling to pieces. Hence, he decided, it needed to be demolished: and he set about planning the new, rational museum-like structure in its place. It was for Descartes, as it has been for us ever since, a question of foundations. Descartes thought that the structure of knowledge developed by medieval philosophy rested on insecure foundations: on principles which might indeed be true, but which were held for no good reason. The lack of good or convincing reasons for holding the principles affected the stability of the whole structure. It was no good tinkering here and there to prevent this or that bit falling down: what we had to do was to demolish the medieval structure and dig down to firm rock, to those principles that no-one in their right mind could doubt, and then build up a new and different structure in accordance with them.

One crucial difference, then, between modern philosophy and medieval philosophy is a negative one: medieval philosophers are not in the least interested in what philosophers now call 'the critical problem' – the problem of finding a sure, indubitable foundation for our knowledge. Medieval philosophers are more willing than modern philosophers have been to start off from what ordinary people claim to know: medieval philosophers do not worry, as since Descartes we have had to worry, how we can be sure that we do know what we know.

This is, of course, to the very great advantage of medieval philosophers. No sooner had Descartes come up with his indubitable, self-evident principles than they were doubted by those to whom they were not evident, or by those who could not see that they could be made into a firm foundation for a structure of knowledge. Most leading philosophers since then have come up with a rival set of first principles that, they think, cannot be doubted by any reasonable person. Within a few years those principles are doubted by everyone except a few faithful disciples. As a result, there appear a number of rival schools of philosophy, rival architects, busily building away in different styles on differently chosen parts of the foundations: and meanwhile, the rest of the building is carried away into other sciences.

There are in any case theoretical difficulties about the whole modern project that dates from Descartes. One aspect of it is the distinction between the self-evident, firm foundations and the more tentative structure that is built up on them: the distinction between experience and theory. It is thought that there is a a set of experiences which are given – whether they be clear and distinct rational conceptions, as they were for rationalists such as Descartes, or sense-experiences, as they were for empiricists such as Locke. Even apart from the fact that there is no rational way of settling the dispute between Descartes and the empiricists, philosophers are now beginning to realise that there is no such thing as pure, 'given' experience, which could be used to check theory. All experience is in some sense already interpreted in terms of some theoretical understanding.

This kind of problem, and this kind of distinction, are unknown to medieval thinkers. Thus we should not look for modern 'pure' philosophy in the medieval texts. No doubt there are plenty of bits in medieval philosophy which can be used in answering the typical modern problems: just as there would be plenty of features in the plans of a medieval cathedral which one could incorporate, valuably, in any work one might be doing in the attempt to reconstruct one's own preferred fragment of the ruins of the museum. There is nothing wrong with this, except that it suffers from the pointlessness of the whole project, the pointlessness of fiddling around with bits of the ruins of a museum which can now never be completed. But this is not the way to understand what the medieval architects were trying to do.

Thus we should not think or say that the medieval philosophers were 'good philosophers' or 'bad philosophers'. Both comments, unless very carefully qualified, are false, though one of them is stupid as well. If we mean by 'being a philosopher' what would be meant by that expression nowadays, then the greatest of the medieval philosophers were not philosophers at all. Even the worst of medieval philosophers was not a philosopher in the modern sense: they were just not trying to do what we are doing, either well or badly. They were doing something which was, to my mind at least, far less futile.

We need to take care in speaking of this. Until quite recently, it was a common view that the medieval philosophers were just bad philosophers, in the modern sense. (It may still be common in some circles in the United Kingdom.) As a reaction to this, more sensible people have for some time now been saying that some at least of the great medieval philosophers were very good philosophers indeed. This is less false than the previous view: as we have said, a great deal of light on modern philosophical problems can indeed be found in medieval works. But it is still a mistake: we can use medieval authors as we please, to our profit, but if we want instead really to understand them we have to understand what it was that they were trying to do. This was quite different from what we are trying to do.

A great deal of confusion has been caused by the attack made by Bertrand Russell on medieval philosophers. He claimed that Aquinas, for example, was not a philosopher at all in any sense that 'we' would recognise: 'we', in this context, apparently meaning twentieth-century intellectuals such as Russell and his readers. This kind of remark is open to a sharp and simple reply of *tu quoque*: the same to you with knobs on, as children said when I was at primary school. There is no reason to suppose that medieval philosophers would have recognised people such as Russell as being philosophers in any sense which *they* would have recognised. This, once we try to escape from the childish prejudice that our present age must be better than any other simply because we happen to live in it – a prejudice which is no more reasonable than a belief that our own country or our own home town must be better than any other because we happen to live in it – leaves us with the realisation that Russell has said very little worth saying. What is worth saying in Russell's comment is that we should not suppose that the intellectual project or projects of modernity are the same as those of the Middle Ages: but it is possible to make this point without assuming a superiority one has no right to.

In any case, the reasons which Russell gives for his conclusion are very faulty. Russell claims that Aquinas was not a philosopher because he was not willing to follow the argument wherever it might lead: Aquinas's Christian faith meant that certain kinds of answer were ruled out in advance: they could not, Aquinas thought, possibly be true. Thus, says Russell, Aquinas was only looking for arguments to back up answers he already held for other reasons: and this, Russell holds, is not part of the task of the philosopher.

Even if we take 'philosopher' in the modern sense, as Russell did, it is clear that Russell is wrong. It often is part of the task of the philosopher to look for good reasons for holding what one already holds: Russell himself, as Kenny remarks in *Aquinas on Mind*, wrote a book of several hundred pages to prove that one plus one equals two. There is nothing wrong with this: and there is nothing wrong with Aquinas's philosophy, either, even from a modern point of view.

It is also instructive to notice the examples Russell gives to support his claim that Aquinas's holding of definite views in advance of the argument shows that he was not a philosopher in the modern sense. The examples he chooses are Aquinas's views on marriage and on the existence of God. These are, as it happens, probably not wholly coincidentally, two questions on which Russell himself had very strong views – very different from those of Aquinas, of course. No amount of argument – and a lot was directed at him – ever convinced Russell that his views on these two questions were mistaken, and he spent a lot of time justifying them or 'looking for arguments to back up what he already held'. It begins to look as if Russell holds that this way of acting is permissible, and even praiseworthy, in a philosopher, always provided that the philosopher, like himself, is in disagreement with the sort of thing the parsons used to say.

It has been a natural reaction among those less prejudiced than Russell – or at least differently prejudiced – to draw attention to these points which can be made against Russell's view. They, quite rightly, draw attention to the enormously valuable contributions to modern philosophy that can be gleaned from reading medieval authors. But though this is natural, it is not the right way to understand medieval philosophy. The reader will be asking, 'then what is the right way?' But before we can answer this we need to look at a simpler question.

1.2 WHAT ARE THE MIDDLE AGES?

The term 'Middle Ages' is a vague one: it can only mean 'the ages that are in the middle, neither ancient nor modern'. This would seem to give us a range from the fall of the Roman Empire in the west until the present day. But historians see a shift in attitudes, the beginning of the 'modern' period, around the time of the fifteenth and sixteenth centuries: so the fall of Byzantium in 1453 is, for the general historian, as good a point to close the medieval period as any. (Though I take it that no serious historian would treat this as more than a conventional date, and perhaps not a particularly helpful one. I have the impression that contemporary historians are far more interested in observing continuities than in discovering possible points to mark breaks in continuity.) At the other end, historians of Western Europe often want to mark off the beginning of the medieval period with the end of what used to be called the Dark Ages: a period in which the historian needs a different set of techniques, owing to the lack of stability in society and the scarcity of records during it. Perhaps 800, the time of Charlemagne, would be a good start for the medieval period: or, if you prefer, the year 1000, by which time the last assault on Western European civilisation from alien barbarians, the Vikings, had been beaten off or assimilated.

These boundaries are easy enough to provide, but none is adequate to define the period in which there existed what must be studied as part of 'medieval philosophy'. We have to start in the fourth century AD, with St Augustine, at the latest. It was Augustine who achieved a triumphant synthesis of ancient Greek learning – of ancient philosophy – and the Jewish and Christian traditions which he also espoused, and so set the pattern for a thousand years' intellectual development: an unrivalled achievement, in the West, for someone who claims merely human authority.

The plan of beginning with Augustine will necessarily draw us further back: we will have to glance at least at the Neoplatonists, whom he admired, and therefore also at their master Plato: and when we go on to examine Boethius, who brought Aristotle's logic into the West in the early sixth century, we will have to look back to Aristotle as well. Later on, when first Arabs and then Christians rediscover the rest of Aristotle's works, in the twelfth and thirteenth centuries, we will have return to Aristotle, to look with more care at other features of his thought.

So much for the beginning: we start medieval philosophy in the fourth century AD, with frequent glances back to the fourth century BC. Where do we end?

This is one of those questions that is unexpectedly easy to answer: as the reader may already have guessed, we finish at Descartes. With Descartes a new approach to knowledge enters, and the modern age begins. We can perhaps regard the Spanish political thinkers of the sixteenth century – for example, Vitoria – as the last philosophers in the medieval style. Even though there is some continuity of teaching after this – even though, for example, there is practically nothing in Locke that could not be found in one medieval philosopher or another – the difference in attitude to that teaching, to the task of the philosopher in general, has already come about by Locke's time. For Locke as for Descartes, we find that the typically modern preoccupations are central: the question of how we know that we know, the question of the foundations of knowledge, and the distinction between what is given in experience and what is a theory constructed on that experience, are at the core of Locke's work. It is hardly an exaggeration to say that there was no more philosophy of any interest done in the traditional manner from Descartes' time until there was some kind of a revival in the nineteenth century.

1.3 WHAT IS AN INTRODUCTION?

That is, what am I doing in this book? It is easier to begin by saying what I am not doing. I do not intend, as can be seen from the above, to show how medieval writings can be made to contribute to current philosophical debates. That has its value, but it is not my task. An easier and perhaps, for most readers, a more useful task would be to set myself to give a brief chronological survey of those writers in the Middle Ages who we can call philosophers. But this, though informative, would also be something of a mistake.

It would be a mistake, firstly, because it would have to take for granted some definite standard of who can be called philosophers. How would I choose which writers to speak about? I could choose only those who called themselves philosophers: but this would be foolish, as it would, in effect, limit the study to those who taught in universities in the faculties of Arts. Most of the greatest thinkers of the medieval universities taught in the faculty of Theology. This criterion of 'being a philosopher' would rule out Aquinas, for example: and there can be no doubt that such a book, an introduction to medieval philosophy with no mention of Aquinas, would be a fraud.

Should I then instead extend my study to all those, whatever they called themselves, who wrote on what would now be called philosophical problems? It may well turn out that this is what has to be done. But not without some consideration: we should not just take it for granted that these are the only authors that can interest us. This is because to do this would also be to take it for granted that our current conception of philosophy is the only one worth accepting. It would not be an introduction, but an interpretation: an interpretation of medieval writers as being the same as modern philosophers, with the same aims, only older.

All history is interpretation, they say: and the briefer the book is the more interpretation there must be: but I see no reason why we should adopt what must certainly be a misinterpretation, and certainly no reason why we should adopt it without even drawing attention to it. Even a list of writers, which mentioned their works and the topics they wrote on, would be something of a misinterpretation: almost certainly the criteria on which the list was drawn up would be modern ones which are foreign to what the thinkers who appear on the list were trying to do.

1.3.1 *The Introduction as a Guidebook*

What needs to be done, in a nutshell, is to introduce the reader to the medieval philosophers, in much the same way as the writer of a travel book tries to introduce readers to the inhabitants of the countries they are reading about.

The past, it is said, is another country. The usefulness of this comparison is lessened for us a little by the fact that when we go to a foreign country nowadays we can expect to find at least parts of it very much like our own. Perhaps there are no completely foreign countries any more. Certainly the anthropologists now think so: no matter how far they travel, it is said, they always find that a Coca-Cola salesman has got there before them. There is no culture at present that is completely alien to us.

But the culture of the past is alien to us, and we need to realise this. We need especially to realise this in the case of our own past. There is so much that is familiar: much of the landscape, some of the buildings, usually at least some elements of the language. We have a tendency to think that our forefathers are just ourselves in funny clothes and haircuts. This is an error. It is the same error as that of a visitor to a foreign country who thinks that just because the people there run the same sort of hotels, and smoke the same kind of tobacco, that he is used to, they must be really the same as he is inside.

Most people who have travelled may have had the experience of a sudden shock which makes them realise that the cosy idea they had before, that a foreign culture is really substantially identical with their own, is utterly mistaken. They are lucky to get this shock: there are people who never feel it. In the case of the past it is harder for us to get the shock. We cannot live among our forefathers in every aspect of their life: we cannot see how their alien thought is reflected in action. We read their thought: but as we read we interpret. It is almost certain that at the start we will misinterpret it: that we will, for example, misunderstand medieval philosophy in much the same way that a visitor staying at hotels in a foreign country will misunderstand his hosts. But if the visitor leaves the hotel and visits the market, if he tries at least to learn the language, if he visits people in their homes, sooner or later the shock will come that will shake him out of his misunderstanding. We cannot do this when we read medieval philosophy.

Perhaps we could: perhaps we could study medieval philosophy only as a part of a study of medieval culture in general. This must be impossible for many students: and even if it were possible, they would not even then be free from the danger of misinterpretation. Everything that is strange can be interpreted in a familiar way, or at least ignored. There may never come the hard shock of the unfamiliar: or at least, it may not come within the confines of a course of study. The unfortunate student will then be like those visitors who are full of knowledge about the place they are visiting, but have no understanding: people who know everything except how the locals see it all.

If visitors are wise they will have consulted books about the country they visiting. These books, if intelligently written, will explain to intending travellers what they are about to see: so that they can really see it, and not pass it over without noticing; or see without understanding, or understand in the wrong way. The purpose of this book is that of an intelligent guidebook to the habits and manners of the fascinating and foreign inhabitants of the realm of medieval philosophy.

The purpose of such a book is to open the imagination: to get visitors to see that what appears strange may be familiar, while what appears familiar may really be strange. Above all, the hope is that visitors to the Middle Ages may come to realise that their own familiar attitudes may in fact be more surprising, less reasonable, less intelligible in themselves, than are the attitudes of the natives of the country being visited.

1.3.2 The Guidebook and History

The first thing one should know before visiting a foreign country is its history: not the 'bare facts' which a compatriot of yours might tell you, but how the inhabitants understand their own history. This may well be a question of stories rather than histories in the modern academic sense: it may even be a question of fairy-stories. But to understand these – or at least to know of their existence – is essential.

So what is the heroic story, the history or legend which explains the medieval philosophers? This book is an attempt to state it. It is not a question of academic history, in our sense: medieval people had practically no 'sense of history' in the modern sense. But they did have a sense of being a part of a continuing story. By hearing that story the modern reader may be enabled to join in a serious conversation with medieval thinkers on their own terms.

This does not mean that this book will have a 'historical' rather than a 'philosophical' approach. Historians of philosophy are quite rightly scathing of those philosophers who think that they can enter into a dialogue with medieval thinkers with no preparation, dragging their medieval predecessors into modern debates. It can be done, as I have said: but it is only as valuable as the modern debate is. Those who limit themselves to this necessarily to fail to gain the great advantage of travelling into a foreign country or into the past, that of widening one's perspectives and broadening one's imagination. Naïve modern philosophers of this kind cannot really learn from medieval philosophers, because they only ask them certain sorts of questions. The study of medieval philosophy is really valuable only if it helps you to see that there are other sorts of questions that can be asked.

But the historians are sometimes in no better a situation. They understand medieval thinkers, as the naïve modern philosopher does not: but they often seem to understand them from the outside, as an entomologist might understand a rare class of beetles. They are thus debarred from learning from them, because they never ask them any questions at all. We need to strike a middle course.

I should enter here a warning, which might with profit have come in earlier: this book will have to be an introduction to the study of philosophy in the Christian West. Important figures of eastern tradition, Muslims and Jews such as Avicenna, Averroes, and Maimonides, will come in only in so far as they have an influence on thinking in the west. (This is a very great deal, by the way.) Ignorance means that I cannot make the East the focus of this work: and to try and make it refer to both East and West indifferently would lead, at best, to two small books, and at worst to an unmeaning list of dates and writings. I am sorry that this has to be so: but it is in part made necessary by history. As far as I can make out, while in the medieval period both East and West were open to influences from the ancient world, there is a rather surprising difference of attitude with regard to contemporary works. Muslim and Jewish works were known and esteemed – and criticised – in the Christian West: but there seems to have been much less traffic the other way. The reasons for this cannot be discussed here. But as a result, this book – like nearly every other – has to take the West as its focus.

2

AUTHORITY AND TRADITION

The aim of this book, as has been said, is to tell the reader the stories which make up the culture of medieval philosophy. It is easier to do this than it would be to tell a reader the stories that make up the culture of modern philosophy, because medieval people were themselves aware that it was important to know how to tell a story properly if one wishes to understand one's own place in it. Medieval people knew what it was to receive a story, to understand it, make oneself part of it, and hand it on. The basic concepts we need if we are to understand what this means are those of authority and tradition.

2.1 ARGUMENTS FROM AUTHORITY

When modern philosophers pick up a work of medieval philosophy for the first time one of the things that strike them most is the way in which the medieval authors constantly appeal to authorities. It seems that for medieval thinkers 'Aristotle said so-and-so' or 'Augustine said so-and-so' are good reasons for believing that so-and-so is the case. This at first makes modern philosophers rub their eyes in amazement: it may lead them to make a Russell-style rejection of the whole of the philosophy of the Middle Ages as 'not really philosophy'. This appeal is totally alien to modern philosophy: for us, the fact that so-and-so said such-and-such, whoever so-and-so may be, just does not count as a good reason – does not count as any kind of reason at all – why we should believe that such-and-such is the case.

But things may not be very much better even if the modern philosophical readers are less prejudiced than Russell seemed to be. If they are less prejudiced, they will read on: and they will find that besides the argument for such-and-such based on the authority of so-and-so, there are also what they are inclined to regard as good arguments: perhaps, indeed, very good ones. This may lead them to read further, to become interested in medieval philosophy for the modern-style arguments that they can find in it: and they will thus become accustomed to skip the frequent arguments from authority, or to regard them as being of merely historical interest, as indicating the sources of the writer. In short, they will read the medieval writer as if he were a modern.

This is, of course, a mistake. Medieval people were not very reflective about their own culture and tradition: but one question which is fairly often explicitly discussed is the status and value of arguments from authority. Aquinas, for example, has a discussion of this point when he examines the method and scope of his study at the start of his massive *Summa Theologiae* (First Part, question 1, article 8). The reason for this reflection is not that they had any doubts about value of the authority in general: it is rather that arguments from authority had a different value depending on whether the authority they were based on was human or divine. Hence the discussions.

We find it fairly frequently stated that the argument from a divine authority is the strongest argument of all, while the argument from a human authority is the weakest of all. This is the conclusion that Aquinas comes to: though, interestingly, he cites the human authority of Boethius as an argument in support of the weakness of arguments from human authority. The reason for this distinction is that human minds, even when honestly applied, are quite often mistaken: while God cannot be mistaken. Hence 'Aristotle says such-and-such' is obviously of much less weight than 'God says such-and-such'.

It might be thought that this doctrine gives some support to the attitude of those modern philosophical readers, who just ignore the use of arguments from authority. The argument from human authority is, even to the medieval reader, the weakest of all: are modern philosophical readers of medieval authors not justified in regarding this argument as so weak as to be negligible? Moreover, modern philosophers probably do not believe in God, or even if they do, they may have very different ideas about what God may be supposed to have said from the ideas medieval people had: are they not then entitled to regard what medieval people thought of as the voice of God as being a merely human voice, the voice of Isaiah or St Paul, and accordingly entitled to treat it as a human authority, the weakest argument, which modern philosophers regard as negligible?

Other modern philosophers will no doubt judge that such modern readers of medieval philosophy are so entitled: and maybe morally they have that right. But it is certain that if they do read medieval writings in this way they are misunderstanding them. For modern intellectuals the voice of authority is no argument at all: for medieval thinkers it was an argument. Admittedly it was the weakest argument of all, so that any other argument was stronger: but it was none the less an argument. You needed another argument to refute it, before you could ignore it. Modern intellectuals think they can just ignore it without any other argument.

For medieval people, if Aristotle said that centaurs did not exist, and one had no stronger reason for believing that centaurs did exist – for example, the evidence of one's own senses – then one had good reason for believing that centaurs did not exist. The existence of this statement of authority meant that 'Do centaurs exist?' was not purely an open question: since there was an authority that had spoken on the subject, the burden of proof and the form of the question were established. Modern readers understand the medieval position, that the argument from authority is the weakest of all, as a polite understatement for their own position, that the argument from authority is no argument at all. This is not what the medieval authors meant: they meant what they said, that it was an argument, even though any other form of argument was stronger.

There are complications, of course. There is the question of the interpretation of the authority: what exactly did Aristotle, say, mean when he said that such-and-such was the case? The fact that every statement needs to be interpreted in the correct way meant, in practice, that it was almost never necessary straightforwardly to contradict an authority. Even if you had seen a centaur, you need not say that Aristotle was wrong: you might argue that Aristotle must have meant something slightly different from the obvious sense of his words.

No-one would be likely to worry about contradicting Aristotle in such a trivial case, of course: but the possibility always existed. This made it possible to blur in practice the important theoretical distinction which has been referred to, between the different strengths of divine and human authority. You could never straightforwardly contradict or deny a thesis which had divine authority behind it: that, medieval thinkers considered, surely rightly, would have been unreasonable. The argument from divine authority was stronger than any other, as Aquinas and others concluded. But what was the correct interpretation of the statements made with divine authority?

The answer to that question rested on human authority, usually: the usual or obvious interpretation of scripture had been made by some human being at some time: it might typically derive from St Augustine. But the argument from Augustine's authority, that this interpretation is in fact the correct interpretation of scripture, is an argument from human authority: it is thus the weakest of all arguments, vulnerable to any other argument.

Thus, for example, the Bible tells us that King Solomon made a large round vessel for the Temple, a vessel which measured ten cubits across and thirty cubits round. The natural interpretation of this passage implies that π, the ratio between the diameter of a circle and its circumference, is three. Probably no figure respected as an authority by thinkers of the Middle Ages ever upheld this natural interpretation: certainly Augustine would not have done. But if any had upheld this interpretation, the human authority of that writer, which would be an argument in favour of this interpretation, would have been vulnerable to stronger arguments drawn from the science of geometry. Thinkers of the Middle Ages knew that π is not three, and so would have claimed that the natural, literal interpretation of God's authoritative statement must be rejected, despite any argument from human authority in favour of that interpretation. The interpretation of this passage in the Bible must be such that we take it to be giving only rough measurements. The argument from God's authority is the strongest of all: it is invulnerable to any other argument. But the argument from the human authority, which might be brought in favour of the literal interpretation, is the weakest of all arguments: it is vulnerable to any other argument, let alone one as strong as a proof of geometry.

The medieval attitude to authority, then, was different from ours. Do we just have to accept this as a brute fact, or can we come to have some imaginative grasp of what it meant to have this different attitude? Can we even come to understand it, to see that it is at least not totally unreasonable or superstitious, as modern philosophers would tend to regard it?

2.2 THE NEED FOR AUTHORITY

The task is a difficult one, but something can be done. Perhaps what should be done is to try and make modern readers understand just how odd our own modern attitude to authority is. Let us begin with an illustration of that attitude. Students of philosophy, in English-speaking countries at least, will know how their tutors will allege that even if we grant that God has indeed spoken and has told us that such-and-such a kind of action is bad, this fact is not in itself a good reason for avoiding that kind of action. We would have to judge whether believing God was itself a good thing. Most students, in my experience, swallow that kind of comment without objection. The task before us here is to explain just how strange that remark would sound to a medieval.

Authority functions in modern society, but its role is practically ignored. We never speak of it: nevertheless, it is in fact by the application of authority that we have learnt almost everything we know that is worth knowing: that is, all the things that we learnt before we went to school. We learnt our language, our family relationships and history, and our culture from our parents. That is, we learned from them almost everything which makes us the people that we are. If we had been spirited away to another family, in another culture, we would have been brought up differently, and been – to the extent that this is possible – different sorts of people.

This teaching was authoritative. We were told that so-and-so is the case, or that in our family we don't do such and such: and we believed what we were told, and acted accordingly. This is what it is to obey authority. We had no reason for believing otherwise, or acting otherwise – how could we have, at that age? – and so we obeyed the authority.

It is important to notice that without some such teaching, without some acceptance of authority, we would not have been capable of achieving the full range of activities that are characteristic of human beings. We could have achieved that full range of characteristically human activities had we been brought up under the authority of a different culture: but without some authority we would not have been brought up, would not have developed into normal, complete human beings at all.

But we grew up. We learnt – from authority, of course – what it is to have reasons for believing, or reasons for acting. As a result, we sometimes had reasons for not believing what we were told on authority – reasons that were, or at least seemed, stronger than the reason which authority supplied. This was and is a reasonable position. It is the position which medieval thinkers upheld, that an argument from authority was an argument, but a rather weak one. This, I would like to maintain, is the position which we all do in fact hold. We are told something, and we believe it, unless we have good reasons for not doing so. We are told to do something, and we do it, unless we have reasons for not doing it. It can happen that people will do appalling things at the bidding of those they see as in authority. For example, in a series of notorious experiments subjects were persuaded by a 'scientist' to administer, as they thought, severe electric shocks to others – despite having the strongest possible reasons for refusing. Though few of us have had the misfortune to be placed in the situation of these experimental subjects, we in fact live

21

like this: it would be good if we understood it better and understood what counts as a good reason for going against authority.

But the really surprising thing about our culture – one of the many that would immediately strike a fully alien ethnologist – is that we pretend that this is not so. There is no reflection on the role of authority in our culture: no discussion of how far it is reasonable to follow it, and what arguments are needed to justify going against it. Instead we pretend that it does not count at all. It has been mentioned that the medieval attitude to authority is something of an exception in cultural attitudes, in that it was not unconscious, but explicit. Our attitude is unconscious: but what is strange about it is that it consists in ignoring the immense part authority in fact plays in our lives.

Authority is used in the education of all of us: but we practically never speak of it. If we do speak of it, it is as a second-best: something that we have to use with children, unfortunately, because their ignorance and weakness mean that no arguments can be used on them. But, we think, authority should be superseded as soon as possible, and replaced by pure reason. No-one should ever believe anything, we think, or act in a particular way, unless they can see good reason for doing so. The fact that believing or acting in such-and-such a way is enjoined by some authority, whether divine or human, does not count as a good reason at all.

This seems to me crazy, and would have seemed crazy to any medieval. All of us have to believe and act without thinking out good reasons most of the time: even when we do have time to think out good reasons we certainly cannot think out each time why those reasons count as good reasons: and, philosophers are now beginning to realise, we cannot really think out why what we count as good reasons do count as good reasons. Descartes thought we could, but the project of Descartes and of his heirs has failed: you cannot rationally justify the rational justifications for action.

As a matter of fact, then, we must all believe or act on authority or custom nearly all the time. This means that by modern standards we scarcely ever believe or act on good reasons. We are thus worse off than were people in the Middle Ages. They accepted authority as giving a good reason for believing or acting, though this reason could be outweighed by other, better reasons. Thus they thought that they were acting reasonably, which is always an advantage. In this case they were able to apply reasonable standards to correct their views and actions: they were able to reflect, reasonably, on authority, and sometimes go against it for good reason. We are in a far worse position. We do not accept that it is reasonable to believe or act on authority: but when we reject authority, we are faced with the impossible task of working things out from the first principles of reason. We are forced into a choice between believing or acting unreasonably, as we think, by following tradition, and believing or acting reasonably by going back to first principles, to the 'given'. We cannot go back to first principles: so we very seldom even perform the modest amount of reasonable checking of authority and custom which were carried out by thinkers in the Middle Ages.

It begins to look as if the first curious difference between our culture and that of the Middle Ages – that of the different attitudes to authority – rests on something curious in our culture rather than on something curious in theirs. What needs explaining is not their acknowledgment of authority, but our rejection or ignoring of it. It begins to look as if the guide-book for intelligent visitors should try to explain to readers why they are themselves so strange. The medieval attitude is strange to us: but, even by our own standards, it does not need as much explaining as our own attitude does.

Perhaps this task of explanation of the readers to themselves is beyond the scope of the guide-book. But it is not beyond its scope to help to evoke in readers a sympathetic attitude to medieval thought: and if it can do this by shaking their conviction that they are themselves the norm, and that the people of the Middle Ages are really rather funny (as, until one is taught otherwise, one tends to regard foreigners), then something will have been achieved.

The thinkers of the Middle Ages would have found the modern opposition between reason and authority quite incomprehensible. If reason is opposed to authority, they would object to us moderns, then why do we not at least try, in so far as possible, to use pure reason in bringing up children? Or if authority is good enough to assure our children's future, why do we not acknowledge it as a guide to our own present? We do in fact use authority as a guide to our own action: surely it must be a mistake to refuse to reflect on it, in the name of a fabulous pure reason. Thinkers of the Middle Ages did rely on authority, and reflected on it: they regarded this as only reasonable. They would have thought, surely rightly, that if they had not been initiated into a community within which reason could develop, by obedience to authority, they would not have been reasonable at all: for being reasonable is one of those characteristically human activities of which we have spoken.

2.3 AUTHORITY, COMMUNITY AND TRADITION

When we were children, we were brought up under authority. This teaching made us what we are: it introduced us into our community: into our family, into our nation, into the human race (considered as a social phenomenon) as full and active members. There are two things to be noticed here. The first is that we needed to be introduced: we could not have attained this status on our own. We were made into full members of the club. We had, no doubt, a right to be made members of the club, in virtue of our birth into this species: but without our upbringing, and the use of authority in this upbringing, this right would never have been exercised.

The other thing to notice is that this community is not just the community of those now living. My great-grandparents were dead before I was born: but part of what I am I owe to them, physically, psychologically and culturally. Despite all the generation gaps that exist or have existed, what we learn on the authority of our parents about who we are, about what to believe or do, is substantially the same as what they learnt from theirs. The differences which we know to exist between the attitudes of different generations are only noticeable because they stand out against a background of agreement. This is what it is for a culture to exist. It is passed on by authority, and it continues through time by tradition: what is passed on by the authority of a parent generation is mostly passed on by the authority of the child generation to its children.

But nowadays, in the West at least, we never speak of this. Tradition, like authority, is seen as very much a second-best: something to be superseded: something, perhaps, that is necessary in childhood, or in past centuries, but not at all to be welcomed by adults of today. Instead, we say, we should trust in reason.

To see through the fallacy involved in this popular slogan we should notice the fact that if we are to trust in reason we need to know what the standards of reasonableness are. We do in fact have standards of reasonableness, as the little child does not. That is why we have to use tradition and authority in teaching children: there can be no dispute about this. But what is seldom noticed nowadays is that we have standards of reasonableness because we have been initiated into our culture by means of tradition and authority. Once we have the standards of reasonableness, we can challenge this or that part of traditional authoritative teaching in the name of these standards of reasonableness: that is, we can challenge doubtful parts of the tradition in the name of more basic parts – perhaps, in the name of the tradition as a whole. But we cannot use part of the tradition to challenge the tradition as a whole: we cannot claim that it is unreasonable to hold to any tradition, when the very standards of reasonableness which we are employing in this challenge only come to us from tradition. It would be like saying that it is impossible to speak one's own language, in one's own language.

It should be noticed that what I am myself doing here is precisely issuing a challenge to one part of our culture in the name of the standards of reasonableness that form another part of it. I am challenging our modern attitude to tradition, because it is not reasonable, and I make the challenge in the name of the standards of reasonableness that I hold as the fruit of tradition. This seems itself a reasonable challenge. What I could not do is challenge our modern culture as a whole for being unreasonable as a whole, because my standards of reasonableness derive from the tradition of this culture, with a little help from reflection on ancient and medieval culture. The modern opposition between tradition and reason is as unreasonable as a universal attack on the unreasonableness of modern culture as a whole would be.

It is hard to re-create the medieval traditional culture as a whole: it is even hard for us to understand what it is to be initiated into such a culture, in which tradition was whole-heartedly accepted. What we can do is to speak of a couple of key aspects of the medieval

25

tradition. The first is the medieval religious tradition, which is of great importance to medieval culture in general, and may, please God, be in some way familiar to at least some readers today: and the other is the medieval tradition of learning.

2.4 COMMUNITY OF FAITH AND COMMUNITY OF LEARNING

Authority is used, it has been said, to introduce the newcomer – typically the child – into a community, a community with a past towards which it typically has a determined attitude. The newcomers accept the authority – they have not yet acquired the standards within the community by which the statements of authority can be judged – and learn the beliefs, attitudes, standards and behaviour which are appropriate to members of that community.

We can see this clearly in the case of a child being brought up in, or an adult being initiated into, a community defined by a shared religious belief. In the case of the religions with which we are most familiar, and which are of most importance to a study of the medieval period the authority is, ultimately, God's authority. This is what is distinctive about Judaism, Christianity and Islam: they go back to an alleged revelation by God. This is, of course, important: it immensely strengthens any statement by authority, as we have mentioned, since God, in these traditions, unlike human beings, can neither be deceived nor deceive others. Historically, the fact that medieval thinkers were part of a religious culture in which a divine authority is believed to be active may go some way to explaining why these medieval thinkers had a more fortunate and intelligent attitude to authority and tradition than we have.

We are less fortunate than medieval thinkers, but we are in some ways their heirs, as they were the heirs of these religious traditions: so the idea is familiar to us. But we should dwell on what it means really to believe this. It is not just that God has appeared, to work a miracle, or to be worshipped, or to found a race of kings, as happens in pagan mythologies. It is, rather, that the one and only God, the God who made all the universe and keeps it in existence from one moment to the next, has intervened in a decisive way in the lives of all rational beings on this earth: He proclaimed a law and offered eternal favour to those who fulfilled that law. Small wonder, then, that the people of the Middle Ages had a higher regard for authority than we have. For they believed that besides all human authorities there was a divine authority. Human authorities can err – but it is still reasonable to trust them. But God as an authority cannot err: what God says is true. If God says that such-and-such a thing is good, then it is good. We are right to trust even in human authorities, to the extent that they are worthy of trust. We are therefore right to trust infinitely in God's authority.

It was at an historical moment, or at more than one, that God spoke. This is itself an important difference from pagan religion. But that historical moment, by the time of the Middle Ages, was long since past: how had it come down to believers? By being handed down by former believers in that authority. Tradition and authority are here inter-woven so closely that they can scarcely be separated: but they are still two different concepts that it is worth trying to distinguish in some way.

The authority is God's authority: but it only comes to the believer through tradition. One thus needs to accept the authority of the tradition as well. One may believe that God will protect those whose task it is to hand down the tradition, so that they will not fall into the errors to which human beings are so prone: but it is only because one accepts the teaching of tradition, which says that God has promised that the tradition will be protected, that one believes that the tradition is so protected. That is, as a matter of logic, one claims that one is right to believe the tradition because to believe the tradition is to believe God: but as a matter of one's own psychological history, one only believes that the authority of God can be found in the tradition because one has come to trust the authority of the tradition that says that it bears the authority of God.

The fact that the tradition itself teaches that the tradition is protected from erring in essentials in passing on God's revelation does not mean that there can be no criticism of what is taught. It is not clear what is essential and what is inessential, in which error could have crept in. We are back at the question discussed above, about the difference between what God has said and what is the

27

correct interpretation of what God has said: at the question about the difference between divine authority and human authority. In the generation in which some members of a tradition are living, error may be creeping into the interpretation of God's message: and it may be up to those members to correct it. It may be that they are the instruments that God wishes to use to preserve the correct tradition. Thus they can criticise individual features of the tradition as they have received it: but they can only do so in the name of the standards which the tradition has handed down to them. They cannot get outside the tradition to criticise it as a whole: if they do so, it means that they have adopted other standards. And why should alien standards be of any value in criticising their own tradition? Especially if the standards of their tradition are supposed to have the authority of God.

This was the situation of the medieval believer, as it is the situation of modern believers – if they are lucky. They had accepted the authority of a tradition, and had been accepted into the community which that tradition defined. They thus believed what that tradition taught, adopted the attitudes that the tradition embodied, and acted as the tradition told them to.

But one need not hold that a tradition enshrines a divine authority to be justified in respecting tradition. There have been many traditional societies: and it is possible to argue that even our own is in some respects really a traditional society without knowing it. A clear example of a non-religious traditional community is the community of learning outlined by Plato and Aristotle. To become a learned person – a philosopher – is for them a process that involves admitting the authority of the philosophical tradition, involves accepting the attitudes, beliefs, behaviour and standards of that community. These attitudes include attitudes to the history of that community, and hence attitudes to the tradition itself. Like the traditional reasonableness of the human race, and like the religious traditions referred to above, such a tradition has its own standards, which are also accepted on the authority of tradition. These can be used to judge individual parts of the tradition, or individual features of the present state of the tradition in this generation, which may be found to be defective in one way or another. But of course the tradition as a whole cannot be judged as not up to standard by the standards of that tradition. It could only be so judged by outside standards: and it is not at all surprising that those with different standards should judge it badly. But they are likely to misunderstand it: as much as we misunderstand the thought of the Middle Ages. There are no neutral standards.

(People have sometimes wondered about how such authoritarian systems can have arisen from the very free-and-easy, questioning, even sceptical philosophising of Socrates. The answer is not simple. Firstly, when we think of Socrates, we are usually thinking of Plato's Socrates: the real Socrates may have been rather different. Plato's Socrates seems to have been intended by him as a device to crack complacency and to make readers willing to submit to the need of being authoritatively taught. There seem to have been more sceptical and doubtful heirs of Socrates, but scepticism is essentially a lonely philosophy, one that does not lend itself to developing a school. Be that as it may, what people might like to consider the 'Socratic' element in Greek philosophy did not survive down to the Middle Ages; though, with the help of some of Aristotle's works, in the Middle Ages they re-invented the dialogue as a mode of philosophising: see below, chapter 3.)

We can, if we wish, compare with the tradition of learning as understood by Plato and Aristotle the tradition of the scientific community in our own day. This is perhaps the nearest we come in our society to a community based on a genuine tradition. The truth about this is disguised from us by the rhetoric used by scientists and philosophers of science about 'reason': but in fact the scientific community is a traditional one, based on authority. Those who wish to enter it have to give up whatever other beliefs, standards and attitudes they may have had, and adopt, on authority, the new standards of the scientific tradition. They cannot hope to justify the beliefs, attitudes and standards of science by means of beliefs, attitudes and standards which they bring from outside. Among these attitudes, it is important to notice, is an attitude towards the scientific tradition itself: an attitude to the history, or rather the story of science. The story of the scientific tradition which the newcomer must accept is not a detailed history of everything that any scientist has ever done in the name of science: it is a genuine tradition, a story which picks out only those things which are to be believed at the present day, or have in some way contributed to what is believed at the present day. This is very much the same as the way in which newcomers into a religious tradition are not told about all the heresies there have been: they are told the faith. Once newcomers have established themselves in the scientific community, they may use the standards of science to correct this or that current or recently past view: but they cannot use the standards of science to overthrow science.

The medieval philosopher was a member of two communities, of each of these kinds. He was a member of a community based on a religious tradition, and he was a member of a community of learning. It is impossible here to discuss whether the notion of a traditional community of learning came down from the ancients, or was carried across from the community of the religious tradition. It might also, as I will partly discuss later, have been carried across from another traditional feature of medieval society: that of the tradition of a craft. No doubt some such story is true. What is important for us to notice here is that the medieval philosopher inhabited a tradition, however the tradition came about: he had a cast of thought according to which the appeal to authority was indeed an argument, though a defeasible one, one that could be defeated by a better or more powerful argument.

How defeasible was it? This brings us back to the question of human authority as opposed to divine authority: but we are perhaps now in a better position to avoid misunderstandings that may easily arise when we consider this question. Medieval thinkers, as we have said, were aware of the difference between human authority and divine authority: but this does not mean that we should hold, as some have done, that they were aware of some form of the modern opposition between faith and reason. They knew that some truths – some of the most important ones – could not be reached by the exercise of a human being's unaided reason. These truths needed to be revealed by God. There were many truths, too, they held, which the unaided human reason could theoretically reach, but which no-one was likely to reach, because of ordinary human weakness. Some of these truths, too, God had revealed. But in the circumstances – by the standards of the tradition – it was reasonable, it was precisely part of the exercise of reason, to believe what God revealed. There was a distinction to be made between faith and reason, but no opposition. It is only in moments of crisis and degeneration in medieval philosophy that we find some authors making such an opposition.

They did not regard the whole of the knowledge they had, then, whether divine or human in origin, as a single mass. There were distinctions to be made, too, both within human knowledge, and within divinely revealed knowledge. One such distinction within human knowledge has just been referred to: the distinction between what human beings could know by the light of their own reason alone in ideal circumstances – in Christian tradition at least, before the Fall – and what could in fact be known by weak, imperfect, sinful and confused human beings like ourselves. In the light of this distinction, it seemed reasonable to medieval philosophers and theologians to hold that it was possible to discover that God exists merely by the exercise of the reason, and at the same time to hold that most people – perhaps everyone – would be too careless, busy, uneducated or preoccupied to work it out. The result is the phenomenon of which they were as well aware as we are, that most believers believe in God on faith – that is, on trust in authority.

Equally, there was a distinction to be made within the knowledge that God communicates to human beings. The knowledge that God communicates to us by faith in this life cannot be compared with the full knowledge that God has promised to communicate in the next life to those who respond to divine grace in this life. The importance of these two distinctions is that they led medieval thinkers to hold that even their dearly loved tradition is imperfect: even if it contains nothing that is false, it cannot expect, in the conditions of fallen humanity in this life, to achieve all truth. Even its standards may be imperfect. Medieval thinkers, therefore, did not and could not believe in the rationalist, Cartesian dream of a perfect system of complete knowledge which could be worked out in the generations of human life on earth. The ultimate standards by which their tradition, however perfectly developed, was to be judged, were not of this world. But at the same time they could not reject all traditions and all standards as equally partial, equally imperfect: they believed that a perfect standard did exist, and that they would be called upon one day to measure up their own developed tradition against it.

Meanwhile life, and study, had to go on. What were the standards by which study or life in the community could be judged as successful, and how could a life, or a work of study, contribute to the life of the tradition?

2.5 THE SOURCES AND STANDARDS OF A TRADITION

A tradition always has a historical origin, even if it is unknown to those in it. What is more important to them is their understanding of their origin. This, a pre-literate traditional culture, will be given – in a set of stories – a mythology. Even if this mythology does not tell of the origin of the culture, it will certainly enshrine that culture's beliefs about what kind of people they are and ought to be. In a literate society this mythology, or set of stories, will take the form of a written text or series of texts: what can be called a canon.

The word 'canon' is taken from the attitudes of Jews and Christians to the texts which their cultures regard as embodying divine authority. But the phenomenon is not confined to communities that claim such authority for their traditions. It is quite clear that the ancient Greeks considered the works of Homer, and to a lesser extent, Hesiod, as being a canon in the sociological sense in which the word is being used here.

What is meant by this is that the works of Homer were seen by the Greeks as having authority. They formed a mirror, as it were, in which the Greeks could look at themselves and understand what they were. They could judge themselves and others by the standards that were enshrined in the attitudes, beliefs, and heroic deeds described in those poems.

2.6 THE DEVELOPMENT OF A CANON THROUGH TRADITION

A canon by its nature is something fixed. But this does not mean that it is entirely static. The understanding of a canon will improve, and reflection on a canon will take place. Little by little these reflections will acquire quasi-canonical status. As the culture whose canon it is continues its life through the generations, there will be those who act according to its standards, and are to be praised: and there will be those who act against its standards and be condemned. In a pre-literate culture these new stories may quite easily be assumed into the canon: but they will not essentially alter it.

What is more interesting is the fact that through the ages the members of the traditional community may come up against new circumstances. These new circumstances will provoke reactions, in accordance with the standards of the canon, which may be unexpected: it may be necessary to take more care in judging of them.

Thus a tradition is not necessarily a static thing: it may, and probably must, develop. It will not be enough for people just to hand on the tradition unchanged, if they are to meet the standards which the tradition itself enjoins. People will need at least to reflect on the application of the standards of the canon to new and different circumstances. That is why, in pre-literate societies at least, the bards were the acknowledged legislators, the interpreters of the canon, and often surrounded by religious sanctions.

Hence, too, we can see how the traditions of the Greeks enshrined in the Homeric canon were commented on, re-interpreted, and applied to new situations, by Aeschylus, Sophocles and Euripides, the great tragedians of the fifth century BC in Athens. These interpretations, for the following century, the century of Plato and Aristotle, were not part of the canon: they did not have full authority. But they had some authority, albeit defeasible, as intelligent reflections on the tradition, and within the tradition. As time went by we see the works of the tragedians becoming canonical: not, indeed, all of them, but certainly those we have today. These are the very works which – archaeology now tells us – were most quoted, most copied, most widespread in the later Greek world. Then they formed the later Greek canon. In time, together with those Romans who reflected on them and interpreted them, these same poets became part of the canon of the governing class in eighteenth- and nineteenth-century Britain.

What was the canon of the Middle Ages? In the first place, there was a sacred canon, the 'canon' in the strict sense, of books that were held to be of God's own writing. The authority these had was divine, and though they could be interpreted, and these interpretations could achieve an authority of their own, nothing could be added to the canon. But there was also a secular canon: which included the poems of Virgil, and as much had come down to them of the ancient philosophers, including Cicero. These also had authority, of a lesser kind: an authority which was merely human and thus defeasible. But their authority still constituted an argument.

The secular canon that these works formed could, theoretically, be added to. Indeed, the most interesting fact in the history of medieval philosophy is that this is just what happened – it was added to. Among the books of the secular canon were to be found the logical works of Aristotle, translated into Latin. As a result, not just these works but Aristotle himself was credited with authority. So when the other works of Aristotle came to the notice of philosophers and other thinkers, it was natural to want to admit them with equal authority to the canon. The problem was that there were already parts of the secular canon, and of the authoritative commentaries of tradition on that canon, which seemed inconsistent with Aristotle. The result was a crisis which almost overthrew the tradition of medieval thought in the west in the thirteenth century, and may be partly blamed for its final overthrow in the sixteenth.

2.7 THE TRADITION OF A CRAFT

Plato and Aristotle, we have said, thought that coming to be a philosopher was a process of being initiated into a tradition. The same is true of the medieval philosophers: the world of learning, for them, was a tradition with its own beliefs, attitudes and standards which newcomers had to accept on authority. As they became initiated, they would acquire the standards which would enable them to understand: but understanding could not be there from the beginning. This tradition bears strong analogies to the traditions of craftsmanship which existed in the Middle Ages: and the people of the Middle Ages were aware of this.

The very name of the faculty of Arts in the university – in which philosophy was studied – bears witness to this, since the name 'art' originally means 'a craft', and was applied metaphorically to the liberal arts. Indeed, the word 'university' is probably an application to the world of learning of the terminology of societies of craftsmen. Then, too, one can see in the structure of the medieval course of studies – reflected still in the degree-ceremonies of many older universities – an analogy to the training of the craftsman. The newcomer to a medieval craft would go through a period of apprenticeship under a master of the craft – answering to the studies required for the Bachelor's Degree. Then the apprentice would qualify as a 'journeyman': a not-yet-fully qualified craftsman who could nevertheless be trusted with some work, under the directions of a master. This corresponds to the period of bachelorhood in the university, while preparing for the Master's Degree, during which the bachelor would undertake minor teaching tasks to prepare younger students for the master's lessons. After the full time of training was complete, the journeyman would qualify as a master in his own right: he would be admitted to the society or guild of masters, alongside his own master, and then had the right to practise the craft without the direction of any other master, and take on apprentices of his own. This answers to a student's graduation as master. The Master's Degree was not an honour conferred on past work, but a licence to begin the practice of a craft. Medieval degrees were more like our driving test or professional qualifications than they are like our modern university degrees.

All this has a number of consequences. In the first place, the new student came to the university to have his attitudes changed, to be made a fit person to enter the community of learning. (This may not have been so much the case in universities such as Bologna, which were considered as communities of students rather than as communities of masters. There the student came with his own attitudes, perhaps, and could expect to keep them through his studies. But it is certainly true of universities set up as communities of masters, such as Paris and others on the Paris model, such as Oxford. It is significant that it was Paris and Oxford that were most renowned for the study of philosophy and theology: Bologna was more famous for the more practical study of the law.) The student had to accept the authority of the masters: he could not hope to be able to judge them or even understand why they taught him what they did before he acquired the standards of the community. In the same way it was the community of craftsmen who were entitled to judge whether work was well or badly done, and whether an apprentice was fit to enter the community of the craft.

Thus the authority of a master, and of the community of masters, was a necessary part of philosophy in the Middle Ages. The community of learning, of the craft, had a definite purpose, as did any craft community: to improve their art according to the best standards they had. These standards were given by authority, and passed down by tradition: but they were also developed by tradition. Those who belonged to the craft, in the succeeding generations, would find themselves surpassing their masters of the preceding generations, according to the standards of those masters. But they would also have to face new situations: the appearance of new materials, for example, would demand the development of a new set of techniques. What is more, by the understanding that they acquired of the standards of the craft as a whole, they would be able to challenge and refine not only techniques but also even some of the previously accepted standards. The tradition of a craft was a living thing: we need only look at the development of architecture through the Middle Ages. The same kind of development, not only of new techniques but even of new standards, occurred in the life of the community of learning.

We can consider the canon of texts as the materials which the learned worked on: the authoritative interpretations of the canon by former masters as the set of techniques and standards of the craft, derived from the practice of former masters. The purpose of the craft – what they were trying to produce – was a perfected craft. They were trying to bring about a philosophy that should be as close as possible to the knowledge of the world which an unfallen Adam and Eve could have reached: and a theology that should be as close as possible to God's own knowledge that is shared by the blessed in heaven. They knew very well that they could never produce the philosophy of the Garden of Eden, and could certainly never reach in this life the standards of the knowledge of the blessed. But their aim was not to produce such systems of knowledge – they knew that God could produce them at any time without their co-operation, and would do so in the next life – but rather to conform the tradition of knowledge on this earth to these models as far as was possible. The system of knowledge on this earth could never be perfect, but it could always be improved, that is, brought nearer perfection: and the more it was improved, the better off the community of learning, and those they served, would be.

2.8 THE AIM OF THE TRADITION AND THE MEANS OF ITS DEVELOPMENT

We have pointed out that newcomers to the craft of learning could not expect to understand everything they were told, much less the reason for everything they were told. Understanding was an aim for the future, which might be achieved more or less fully as a practising master. In the same way, full understanding of its own tradition was a future for the community of the craft of learning as a whole. They could understand much – they thought – as they were: but there would always be obscurities in their system of knowledge until the craft was entirely perfected. This is what they were striving for. And though they knew they might never achieve it, they knew that every step in the perfection of their system of knowledge was a step towards their aim, and an increase in understanding.

The difference here between their attitude and aims and the attitudes and aims of the rationalist projects that stem from Descartes needs stressing. For Descartes and his heirs, we need to start from a firm foundation of basic understanding, and to build up a system of perfect knowledge from those foundations, understanding every step. That is, every step must be understood: and its connection to the immediately understood foundations must be understood as well, from the beginning. The Cartesian system of knowledge may take time to build up: but though it is not complete, every part of it that exists at any time must be perfect, and perfectly understood at that time. For medieval thinkers perfect understanding was something to aim for, something in the future.

The whole system was not only incomplete, it was also imperfect. Perfection, and perfect understanding, could only be achieved when completion was achieved. There could be no question of a perfect understanding from the start, or a perfect understanding of an as yet imperfect and incomplete system.

We might put it this way: for Descartes, only what could be completely understood could be known. So he starts off with the perfectly understood and perfectly known self-evident principles, and tries (and fails) to build up the whole system of knowledge from there. Medieval philosophers were quite happy to start from what they knew, but didn't fully understand. They knew a lot of things, from common sense, from experience, from the teaching of the ancients, and from God's revelation. They did not worry, as Descartes did, about trying to understand how they knew these things: this understanding, they thought, would come little by little, as their system of knowledge became nearer perfection. Hence we might say that Descartes started from what he could understand, and aimed to build up knowledge on this basis: medieval philosophers started from what they knew, and aimed to understand it. As their tradition developed and moved towards its aim of perfection, they would come to understand more and more of what they knew, and also come to know more and more.

The stress which has been laid on the fact that medieval thinkers did not expect their system of knowledge ever to be complete, and hence ever completely understandable, in this life, makes it look as if they subscribed to the proverb 'It is better to travel hopefully than to arrive'. In fact, probably most medieval scholars would have found this proverb almost impossible to understand. What they did hold was that it was better to build hopefully than to do nothing, or to spend all one's time grubbing in the foundations. The cathedral might never be completed: bits of it might collapse or have to be replaced: the plans handed down by a previous generation of builders might turn out to be inadequate: but it was worth while building the cathedral. The analogy is especially apt, as the system of knowledge of the medieval scholars, like the cathedral of the medieval builders, was intended both for the honour of God and for the protection and edification of God's people.

All this led to a modest attitude among medieval scholars. (On a theoretical level, I mean: I expect that vanity and ambition were quite as common among medieval scholars as individuals as they are among academics today.) The medieval scholar was initiated into a tradition at a certain historical moment: he took it as he found it, trusting it. The task before him was that of solving current problems, the problems that had not yet been solved in the tradition. In the same way a builder could be expected, in general, to continue building where others had left off, and not suddenly to go back and start rebuilding parts that had already been built.

It is the same with us today in science: the scientist may wish he had been introduced into science fifty years before or fifty years later, when the tradition might be at a more interesting stage of development: but if he is a scientist at the present day what he has to work on is the problems that present-day science faces.

This means, as has been said, trusting the tradition: trusting that the tradition has got it all more or less right so far. In the same way, the tradition of a craft hands down the craft in its present state, which is taken as the best so far, by the best standards achieved so far. There is no question of going back in search of first principles.

Of course, it may turn out that this is in one case or another a mistake: the tradition may have gone astray: part of the cathedral may well have been badly built and may need rebuilding on new lines before any more can be done. There may be insoluble problems for the philosophical tradition at one moment or another of the Middle Ages, just as there may be insoluble problems at one moment or another in the life of modern science. It may be that at that stage what is needed is to go back and retrace a few false steps: it may even be that the problem reveals to us unsuspected flaws here and there in the very standards of the tradition. Such moments may be rare or frequent: but the need of retracing a few false steps every so often does not do away with the need for trusting the tradition in general. Rather it reinforces it: for the error of parts of the tradition can only be judged by reference to the tradition as a whole.

The stages in the development of the tradition can thus be seen as stages in a dialogue. In each stage, one of the parties in the dialogue is the tradition itself: the other is the master who is conducting this stage of the dialogue. The teaching of the tradition is examined: does it contain any unresolved contradictions? Have recent developments in the tradition cast either light or doubt on what has gone before? Have the problems posed to the tradition in recent generations been successfully resolved? Could they be resolved any better? The master is expected to be able to provide some kind of answer to all these questions, and to hand on the tradition to his pupils in a condition which is at least as good as the condition in which he has received it, and he hopes, slightly better. Unlike the contemporary philosopher, he would not feel that he had achieved anything if he had merely presented a whole set of new problems: the new problems which he may expect to have provided for the next generation should be problems that arise out of the resolution of older problems. Medieval masters lived in an atmosphere, ideally, in which they could hope for continual improvement in this way.

It is important to notice that the overthrow of medieval thought, and thus the abandonment of any hope of progress and improvement, occurs when influential figures refuse to trust the tradition, and refuse to work on the problems that the tradition faces in its current state. Medieval philosophical thought is overthrown when Descartes insists on returning to first self-evident principles, and medieval theology is overthrown when Luther rejects the tradition of the Church and announces a return to scripture alone. We can see other minor crises in the history of medieval thought conforming to the same pattern.

2.9 HARMONY AND RECONCILIATION

Trust in the tradition is part of the respectful attitude to authority which we have so often commented on. A consequence of this is the effort put by medieval thinkers into harmonising and reconciling authoritative elements in their tradition. We have seen something of how this effort was made, discussing the correct interpretation of the authorities so that they all support the thesis being argued for. This is not just an act of politeness towards a long-dead author, but an attempt to make all the tradition a single system of knowledge.

2.10 THE HISTORICAL PROCESS
OF THE DEVELOPMENT OF TRADITION

This process, which occurred on a small scale in the discussion of individual theses, occurs on a large scale throughout the history of medieval philosophy. We shall examine this in more detail in the last three chapters of the book: but there the broad lines of the development and improvement of the tradition will have to be overlaid by some details of conflict, crisis and failure. Here we can give an extremely simplified sketch.

The intellectual work of St Augustine – with whom, we said, we have to consider medieval philosophy to have begun – was all such a work of harmonisation and synthesis. The task he set himself was that of harmonising as much of pagan philosophy as could be harmonised with the teachings of Scripture and the Church.

The same task, in different ways, was carried out by the mysterious Syrian monk who wrote under the name of Dionysius the Areopagite (now usually known as Pseudo-Dionysius), and by Boethius. The writings of these three formed the most important elements in the authoritative interpretation of the sacred and secular canons which was handed down in medieval tradition. It is by their standards of these that the great figures that began to appear in the eleventh century, such as Anselm and Abelard, developed their own thoughts. Abelard, as we shall see, went too far in his attempt to develop the tradition, and was rebuked for it in the name of authority. What is important to notice is that he accepted the rebuke.

Meanwhile in the East hitherto unknown texts of Aristotle were coming to the notice of thinkers. There they had their own tradition, with the Koran at the centre of the canon: but the same forces were at work in shaping the tradition. Since in the East, too, Aristotle was respected as an authority, the new texts presented a problem. Could they be harmonised, taken into the canon, and interpreted in accordance with the tradition, or not? If not, which should one reject, the tradition or the authority of the new texts? Some notable thinkers, particularly Avicenna and Averroes, grappled with this problem. At the same time Maimonides, within his own Jewish tradition, was trying to carry out the same task.

It seems that all attempts failed, though perhaps many would say they should have succeeded. Brilliant though they were, they were not accepted by the other custodians of the tradition in the East, and the new works of Aristotle never became a part of that tradition.

When these same works filtered through into the West, the same problem was faced, in an even more difficult form. For, the new texts of Aristotle had already received their interpretation from Avicenna and Averroes, who had sought to make them fit with their own tradition. But to make Aristotle harmonise with Muslim tradition might be precisely to make him yet more inconsistent with Christian tradition.

One of those who faced up to this challenge was St Albert the Great. He devoted his life to giving an accurate interpretation of Aristotle's new works, an interpretation which, shorn of all extra difficulties which the Muslim interpreters had brought in, might be harmonised with the Augustinian, Christian tradition. At the same time he continued to work at his own contribution to developing that tradition. Most of all, however, he is to be admired for having taught one who was capable of achieving that harmonisation: St Thomas Aquinas.

In the index to the latest edition of Aquinas's greatest work, the *Summa Theologiae*, the references to Augustine take up thirty-nine columns, while the references to Aristotle take up thirty-five: more than three times as many as their nearest rival and a clear indication of Aquinas' brilliant reconciliation of the two traditions. He took them both up at the point at which they then stood, with all their current problems. He demonstrated that the Aristotelian tradition alone was unable to solve its own problems, and that the same was true of the Augustinian tradition. In his synthesis, however, the defects of each could be supplemented by the other, and the problems of that generation solved. This, of course, was not intended by Aquinas to be a perfected system of knowledge – it would give rise to problems and clearly stood in need of development at many points – but it was a step towards the complete and perfect understanding which was the aim of the development of tradition.

Alas, the historian must report that, for all its brilliance, Aquinas' harmonisation of traditions in the West was not much more successful than those of Avicenna, Averroes, and Maimonides in the East. Aristotle was not rejected, as to a certain extent he had been in the East: instead, the tradition began to fragment. Theology, the development of the Augustinian tradition, declared its autonomy from philosophy, in the writings of John Duns Scotus. As a natural corollary, philosophy, the development of the Aristotelian tradition, declared its autonomy too. The disastrous effects of this schism were disguised from the thinkers of the time by the fact that the two traditions continued to exist and work in the same establishments: and by the continued success of each party in developing their own traditions. But the traditions were now partial: they had secretly given up the aim of constructing a system which would embrace all knowledge. There continued to be progress and development, particularly in logic and related fields, and in the study of the theory of law: but these developments were no longer developments towards the original aim.

As a result, by the end of the medieval period, there were a number of apparently successful traditions, within each major field of study. But though they were rivals, they were not competing in any real sense: none could offer, and none could even claim, even a partial understanding of the whole of reality which could absorb the knowledge enshrined in the other traditions. And so it went on: until first Luther and then Descartes looked round at the clamour of the rival schools. The rival claims could not be judged in any reasonable way, as there was no over-arching tradition which taught standards which could judge the standards of the different partial traditions: nor was anybody willing to take the trouble to enter into more than one tradition, as Aquinas had done, and attempt to reconcile them both from within. As a result both Luther and Descartes rejected tradition, and sought to go back to the original authority: either Scripture or pure reason. Further, Descartes, faced with the warring partial traditions, each with rival authorities, insisted that the authority should be acceptable to all: should, in fact be evident to all. There was to be no room for trust in authority: every step should be immediately clear to all. The result of this project is the present disastrous state of philosophy: and it all stems from the

the late medieval refusal to accept Aquinas's contribution to the traditional project of reconciling and harmonising authorities.

In the next chapter we will look at an example of the typical form in which the task reconciliation and development that the medieval master set himself was carried out, the form of the *question*, before going on in chapter 4 to examine how and to what extent the ideals outlined in this chapter were in fact achieved.

3

THE *QUESTION*

The medieval attitude of trust in the tradition, of hope for development and improvement through the reconciliation and harmonisation of authorities, is typified and enshrined in the medieval academic form of the inquiry. This was originally a live debate within the university schools. Most of what has come down to us are not literal copies of these debates – called *questions* – but an account of them prepared and refined for publication by the master – or sometimes by one of the students or by the bachelor, perhaps corrected by the master and perhaps not. They took place within all the faculties. Dante has a minor geographical/astronomical work called '*The question of land and sea*', which is an account of a *question* which he presented at the university of Bologna, I believe, in middle age.

The form of the *question is* easier to illustrate than to describe. As an example of the *question*-form I offer an article (a sub-division of a full *question*) from the *Summa Theologiae* of Aquinas (First Part of the Second Part, question 6, article 8). The *Summa* is a text-book, and is not even remotely the record of a live debate in the schools: but Aquinas has decided to keep to the form of the *question*. A real *question* in the schools – and we have a number of accounts of Aquinas's own live *questions* – would be far longer and more difficult for the unfamiliar reader to follow. I shall give the text in full and then go through it in detail, drawing attention to points that seem to me of interest.

The eighth part of the *question* asks, does an agent act involuntarily if he acts in ignorance?

We approach this eighth part in the following way: apparently the ignorance of an agent does not make an action involuntary.

Firstly, because, as St John Damascene says, 'an involuntary action deserves pardon'. But sometimes an action done out of ignorance does not deserve pardon, as we see from the *First Epistle to the Corinthians*, where it says: 'If a man know not, he shall not be known'. Therefore the ignorance of the agent does not make an action involuntary.

Secondly, according to the book of *Proverbs*, every sin is accompanied by ignorance: 'They err that work evil'. So if the ignorance of the agent did make an action involuntary, it would follow that every sin is involuntary. This goes against what St Augustine says: 'Every sin is voluntary'.

Thirdly, according to St John Damascene, involuntary actions are accompanied by distress. But there are some actions that are performed in ignorance but without any distress: for example, if a man were to kill his enemy, whom he wanted to kill, when he thought that he was killing a deer. So the ignorance of the agent does not make an action involuntary.

But against this view we have what both Aristotle and St John Damascene say: that some kinds of involuntary actions are made so by the ignorance of the agent.

The reply: we have to say that the ignorance of the agent can make an action involuntary to the extent that this ignorance is absence of the knowledge which is required to make an action voluntary. This is something we have already discussed. But it is only certain kinds of ignorance that mean the absence of this kind of knowledge. To see this, we have to notice that ignorance in the agent can be related to his willing in three ways: ignorance can accompany willing, it can follow on from willing, or it can precede willing.

Ignorance that accompanies willing means that the agent does not know what is being done, but even if he did know, he would do it all the same. This kind of ignorance does not make the agent will something to occur: it just happens that the action and the ignorance occur together. This is the kind of ignorance we find in the example given above. Someone wants to kill his enemy, and does so, but he does so without knowing it, thinking that he is killing a deer. This kind of ignorance in the agent, as Aristotle says, does not make the action involuntary. This is because it does not make anything happen which the will rejects. What it does is make the action non-voluntary, since the agent could not have willed the action since he did not know he was performing it.

Ignorance that follows on willing is related to the will in the following way: the ignorance itself is something voluntary. We can be voluntarily ignorant in two ways, in the two different ways of doing something voluntarily which we have mentioned above. [These are voluntarily doing something and voluntarily not doing something. In this case, the distinction creates a further one: that between deliberately wanting not to know something, and not having any desire to know something.]

In the first way we are voluntarily ignorant because ignorance is made the object of an act of will. This is the case of someone who deliberately chooses no to know, either in order to have an excuse for his sin, or in order not to have to stop sinning. Compare the book of *Job*, which speaks of those who say to God: 'We do not desire the knowledge of thy ways'. This is called 'affected' ignorance.

The other way in which we can be ignorant voluntarily is by being ignorant of what anyone can and should know. This ignorance is voluntary, in the same way as not wanting and not acting are said to be voluntary, as we said above.

There are two kinds of people who are said to be voluntarily ignorant in this way. The first is someone who does not actually consider what he in fact knows, and can and should consider, whether he does this out of passion or out of some settled disposition. We call this kind ignorance in bad choice. The other is someone who makes no effort to acquire the knowledge that he should have: it is called ignorance of the right as a whole, which is something that he ought to know. He is ignorant voluntarily, because his ignorance arises out of his [voluntary] negligence.

When an agent is voluntarily ignorant in any of the above ways, the fact of his being ignorant does not make the action involuntary in the strict sense [and hence deserving of pardon]. It can be said to make his action involuntary in a looser sense, to the extent that it comes before the desire to perform an action, a desire that would not have arisen if the agent had not been ignorant.

Ignorance that comes before the willing is related to the will in the following way: it is not itself something voluntary, but it makes the agent will something that he would otherwise not have willed. This can happen when an agent is ignorant of some circumstances to do with the action, circumstances which he had no duty to know about, and as a result does something which he would not have done if he had known. An example would be if an archer takes all due precautions, but just does not notice that someone is passing on the path, and shoots his arrow, which kills the passer-by. Being ignorant in this way makes the action involuntary in the strict sense.

From this discussion we can see how to answer the objections made at the start. The first objection has to do with someone's being ignorant of what anyone ought to know. The second has to do with 'ignorance in choice', which, we have said, is itself in some way voluntary. The third objection has to do with ignorance that accompanies an action.

At the beginning Aquinas states the problem, the *question* at issue: 'The eighth part of the *question* asks, does an agent act involuntarily if he acts in ignorance?' The *question* which he, as Master, sets, is not one that he himself has dreamed up: he takes a thesis which is to be found in the tradition and asks whether or not that thesis is true. There are, as we see, authoritative statements both from St John Damascene (a ninth-century Syrian theologian of great authority, especially on moral questions, in which he tried to assimilate Aristotelian concepts into Christian thought) and Aristotle himself, to the effect that an agent who acts in ignorance acts involuntarily. Aristotle – as Aquinas was well aware since, around this time, he was beginning to work on a commentary on Aristotle's *Ethics* – devotes a whole chapter to this discussion at the start of the third book of the *Nicomachean Ethics*.

The thesis has also the additional advantage, for present purposes, of being one that the modern reader will be inclined to accept. 'I didn't know I was doing it' is good support for the claim 'I didn't mean to do it'. The *question* in Aquinas comes in a context in which are discussed further authoritative statements, by the same authors, to the effect that involuntary actions are worthy of pardon. This too is something which we would be inclined to accept. 'I didn't mean to do it' is generally considered as good support for the demand 'Don't blame me for it'.

Aquinas goes on to list three objections to this thesis, reasons why we should decide that the thesis is false:

> We approach this eighth part in the following way: apparently the ignorance of an agent does not make an action involuntary.
>
> Firstly, because, as St John Damascene says, 'an involuntary action deserves pardon'. But sometimes an action done out of ignorance does not deserve pardon, as we see from the *First Epistle to the Corinthians*, where it says: 'If a man know not, he shall not be known'. Therefore the ignorance of the agent does not make an action involuntary.

Secondly, according to the book of *Proverbs*, every sin is accompanied by ignorance: 'They err that work evil'. So if the ignorance of the agent did make an action involuntary, it would follow that every sin is involuntary. This goes against what St Augustine says: 'Every sin is voluntary'.

Thirdly, according to St John Damascene, involuntary actions are accompanied by distress. But there are some actions that are performed in ignorance but without any distress: for example, if a man were to kill his enemy, whom he wanted to kill, when he thought that he was killing a deer. so the ignorance of the agent does not make an action involuntary.

All these objections, arguments against the thesis, are based on authority. This need not always be the case. Aquinas himself often uses other arguments in his objections. In the *Summa*, he usually limits himself to three objections, the strongest he can think of. In a live debate, it was the students, the bachelor and the other masters present who came up with the objections, and they might present dozens of them. As the tradition has developed, arguments against almost any given thesis will have cropped up from time to time.

In a live debate, it would usually be the task of the bachelor, in general, to marshal the objections, make any distinctions between different senses of words and different kinds of argument that might be necessary, and put forward some arguments against the objections. Sometimes he might play off one objection against another. All the distinctions and counter-arguments put forward by the bachelor might themselves be countered. In the schematic summary which is the *Summa* Aquinas usually limits himself to a single counter-argument in favour of the thesis, nearly always giving a plain authoritative statement. Hence here: 'But against this view we have what both Aristotle and St John Damascene say: that some kinds of involuntary actions are made so by the ignorance of the agent.'

After this 'the *question* is determined', as the technical expression had it: the master gives his defence of the thesis. This is intended to be a summing up of the tradition, and to contain the master's own contribution to the development of the tradition. He would be expected to make all the distinctions of sense that might be necessary to interpret the different authoritative statements found in the tradition, in such a way that they could be seen to support the thesis. He also might be expected to bring in new arguments that he had himself developed. Aquinas's 'determination' is of particular interest here.

The reply: we have to say that the ignorance of the agent can make an action involuntary to the extent that this ignorance is absence of the knowledge which is required to make an action voluntary. This is something we have already discussed. But it is only certain kinds of ignorance that mean the absence of this kind of knowledge. To see this, we have to notice that ignorance in the agent can be related to his willing in three ways: ignorance can accompany willing, it can follow on from willing, or it can precede willing.

Ignorance that accompanies willing means that the agent does not know what is being done, but even if he did know, he would do it all the same. This kind of ignorance does not make the agent will something to occur: it just happens that the action and the ignorance occur together. This is the kind of ignorance we find in the example given above. Someone wants to kill his enemy, and does so, but he does so without knowing it, thinking that he is killing a deer. This kind of ignorance in the agent, as Aristotle says, does not make the action involuntary. This is because it does not make anything happen which the will rejects. What it does is make the action non-voluntary, since the agent could not have willed the action since he did not know he was performing it.

Ignorance that follows on willing is related to the will in the following way: the ignorance itself is something voluntary. We can be voluntarily ignorant in two ways, in the two different ways of doing something voluntarily which we have mentioned above. [These are voluntarily doing something and voluntarily not doing something. In this case, the distinction creates a further one: that between deliberately wanting not to know something, and not having any desire to know something.]

In the first way we are voluntarily ignorant because ignorance is made the object of an act of will. This is the case of someone who deliberately chooses not to know, either in order to have an excuse for his sin, or in order not to have to stop sinning. Compare the book of *Job*, which speaks of those who say to God: 'We do not desire the knowledge of thy ways'. This is called 'affected' ignorance.

The other way in which we can be ignorant voluntarily is by being ignorant of what anyone can and should know. This ignorance is voluntary, in the same way as not wanting and not acting are said to be voluntary, as we said above.

There are two kinds of people who are said to be voluntarily ignorant in this way. The first is someone who does not actually consider what he in fact knows, and can and should consider, whether he does this out of passion or out of some settled disposition. We call this kind 'ignorance in bad choice'. The other is someone who makes no effort to acquire the knowledge that he should have: it is called 'ignorance of the right as a whole', which is something that he ought to know. He is ignorant voluntarily, because his ignorance arises out of his [voluntary] negligence.

When an agent is voluntarily ignorant in any of the above ways, the fact of his being ignorant does not make the action involuntary in the strict sense [and hence deserving of pardon]. It can be said to make his action involuntary in a looser sense, to the extent that it comes before the desire to perform an action, a desire that would not have arisen if the agent had not been ignorant.

Ignorance that comes before the willing is related to the will in the following way: it is not itself something voluntary, but it makes the agent will something that he would otherwise not have willed. This can happen when an agent is ignorant of some circumstances to do with the action, circumstances which he had no duty to know about, and as a result does something which he would not have done if he had known. An example would be if an archer takes all due precautions, but just does not notice that someone is passing on the path, and shoots his arrow, which kills the passer-by. Being ignorant in this way makes the action involuntary in the strict sense.

The determination of this *question* is of particular interest in illustrating how the tradition developed. This is not merely because it gives the reader some idea of the flavour of medieval philosophy, in the way in which the determination makes a set of multiple distinctions of kinds of ignorance and kinds of voluntariness, and between strict and loose sense of the word 'voluntary'. (If the typical phrase of English-speaking philosophy in the middle part of this century was 'it all depends what you mean by . . .', the typical phrase of medieval philosophy was 'We should distinguish . . .'.) Beyond that, this determination is a particularly good example of the reconciliation of different authoritative elements in the tradition.

The thesis, that an agent's ignorance can make his action involuntary, comes from Aristotle, from whom St John Damascene probably derives it. We have observed that moderns too are quite likely to be interested in this question, and to relate it, as Aristotle himself does, to the question of whether a person who acts involuntarily through ignorance can be excused from blame. But Aristotle is only interested in the question of praise and blame quite incidentally, while for moderns the question is quite likely to be thought of as a central theme of moral philosophy. What really interests Aristotle is the question of what kinds of actions do, and what kinds of actions do not, count as solid evidence in ascribing to someone a particular settled state of character, a virtue or a vice, an excellence or a defect. Thus Aristotle's answer is going to be straightforward, since e.g. having done something bad unwittingly and thus involuntarily will not count as evidence against ascribing excellence of character.

Where does Aquinas stand on this? There can be little doubt that, unlike Aristotle, he is primarily interested in praise and blame, in guilt and innocence, and thus in 'moral responsibility' as it is called. He, like modern people, is interested in the moral quality of individual actions, rather than in the moral quality of states of character, which is what interested Aristotle. This difference is a consequence of the fact that the Christian religious tradition has inherited from Judaism the concept of morality as a God-given law, a concept which Aristotle entirely lacks. We modern people have the structure of moral thought appropriate to a system of morality which is understood as a God-given law, with the additional problem that most of us have effectively ceased to believe in God as Lawgiver.

It is thus important to notice how Aquinas here brings the Aristotelian discussion into a framework that derives from other elements in the tradition. The concepts of 'ignorance in bad choice' and 'ignorance of the right as a whole' are concepts that Aristotle uses: indeed, these very expressions are literal translations of Aristotle's Greek. But this Aristotelian distinction is placed within an overall framework of a distinction which is made between ignorance that accompanies willing, ignorance that follows on from willing, and ignorance that precedes willing.

A few years later St Thomas was to complete a commentary on the *Nicomachean Ethics*, the work in which Aristotle discusses the connection between ignorance and involuntariness. In that commentary he merely expounds Aristotle: he does not place the discussion, as he does here, in any wider context. He seems to have been aware that Aristotle's own concerns in the passage at issue were slightly different from his own.

Where does the distinction between ignorance that accompanies willing, ignorance that follows on from willing, and ignorance that precedes willing, come from? I have not been able to trace it in any earlier writer, so I shall here presume that it is probably Aquinas's own. I am insufficiently competent in the kind of scholarship which would be necessary to carry through this search, and though the question is an interesting one, the answer to it is fairly irrelevant in this context. What I wish to do here is to draw attention to the way in which this distinction is used to incorporate Aristotle's insights, which arose in a differently-focussed conceptual context, into a framework provided by Christian interests and beliefs, and by philosophical concepts, such as that of the will, which developed after Aristotle's time in the early medieval tradition. If the distinction is indeed Aquinas's own, then it is he who must take the credit for achieving this incorporation, and thus improving the tradition in this respect, by reconciling slightly different authorities. If Aquinas derives the distinction from somewhere else, then perhaps Aquinas still deserves the credit for the use he makes of it. At the least Aquinas deserves credit for having seen the need to pass on a brilliant piece of reconciliation in its entirety. My ignorance here is fairly appropriate to the image we earlier used of medieval learning as a cathedral: the master masons who worked on this or that part of a Gothic cathedral were many, and most are anonymous: yet each contributed to the whole.

By making the distinction Aquinas (or his unknown predecessor) has managed to link the question of ignorance, discussed by Aristotle in the context of character, with the individual action. This is what was needed for the notion of ignorance to be useful in the context of the law-like structure of Christian ethics. The distinction has been achieved by relating ignorance to the will. The concept of the will – of a faculty of wanting – is one that antiquity in general and Aristotle in particular lacked, at least explicitly. It only developed in Christian theological tradition – I believe St John Damascene himself played an important role in this – and was then taken over into the Christian philosophical tradition.

Ignorance is thus seen as making an action involuntary only if it precedes wanting and is instrumental in bringing about that wanting; a wanting which would not otherwise occur. If any of these conditions are absent, then the ignorance of the agent does not make the action involuntary, and thus cannot contribute to taking away the guilt of a bad action thus performed.

Aquinas has thus reconciled three differing elements in the tradition: the idea that ignorance can make an action involuntary, and thus excuse it; the idea, commonly associated with Socrates, which Aquinas would have found criticised in Aristotle (though the authoritative statement of it here is taken from the Bible) that everyone who acts badly is making a mistake, and is thus in some way ignorant of what it is best to do; and the idea that every bad action is blameworthy, and therefore must be voluntary. These last two notions are set out in the authoritative statements that were used in the objections to the thesis, and accordingly Aquinas returns to show how the distinction made in the determination create a framework within which these claims can be, with reservations, admitted.

> From this discussion we can see how to answer the objections made at the start. The first objection has to do with someone's being ignorant of what anyone ought to know. The second has to do with 'ignorance in choice', which, we have said, is itself in some way voluntary. The third objection has to do with ignorance that accompanies an action.

This paragraph, the answers to the objections, forms part of the standard pattern of the *question*. After the Master has made his determination of the *question* he makes a detailed refutation of all the objections that have been brought. He may use different kinds of argument. Often he shows that the objections are based on a wrong interpretation of the authoritative statements used in them. Here, for example, Aquinas points out that once the distinctions have been made, we need not take the remarks of the book of *Proverbs*, of St Paul, St Augustine, and St John Damascene as referring to ignorance in general: we can distinguish the kinds of ignorance about which the statements are true, and the kinds for which they are not true.

This refutation of the objections shows how the tradition has been improved by the master in charge of the *question*. Problems which existed in the tradition have been solved, or, at the least, the correct solution achieved by some previous master has been handed on the the students who were, from their objections, clearly unaware of it. And these students will be the next generation of masters. Some of them will perhaps find problems which are caused by this very solution, when related to solutions to other *questions* achieved in this same generation, or to traditional solutions. It will then be their task to solve the new problems. In this way there was rational grounds for hope that the tradition would be growing ever nearer the perfection at which it was aiming.

4

AUGUSTINE AND THE AUGUSTINIAN TRADITION

The aim of the second part of this book is to show how far the ideals outlined in the first half were in fact achieved, and what concepts were of importance in the tradition that was developed in this way. It is not a full historical survey: it will pay attention only to a few major figures. Readers who are looking for a summary of the life and works of this or that medieval thinker who they may have come across in their reading will have to look elsewhere: typically, at an encyclopedia, or at one of the books cited in the reading list at the end. Nor do I offer a full philosophical survey: the concepts dealt with will be only a few crucial ones which are essential to an understanding of the medieval philosophical system. We begin, in this chapter, with an examination of the thought of St Augustine of Hippo (354–430), and a sketch of the chief features of the tradition that stems from him.

4.1 AUGUSTINE'S THOUGHT IN AUGUSTINE'S LIFE

We have said that medieval philosophy, indeed medieval thought in general, begins with Augustine. Any encyclopedia will explain his achievement as that of bringing about a synthesis between Christian and pagan wisdom: of bringing into the thought of Christians all that could be brought of the culture of his day, and thus, more than any other, laying the foundations for the continuation of learning. This is, in a nutshell, what he achieved: but there is more that could be said.

The impression caused on anyone who reads Augustine's auto-biographical *Confessions* is that of a man whose thought and life were in an extremely close unity. This is a book that should be read by anyone with an interest in the thought of late antiquity, of the Middle Ages, and of Christianity in general: it is full of meat. However, the feature of it that most concerns us here is the way in which the moral and religious development it describes are related to intellectual development. For Augustine, thought and life cannot be separated – or rather, when separated, are a sign of ignorance and depravity.

This belief is itself one that Augustine had arrived at, not as the result of theorising, but as the fruit of the experience of his own life. He came to realise that before his conversion there had been a period in which theoretical understanding failed. This failure arose because of the separation he had allowed to grow up between theory and action. Though he had read Plato and his neo-Platonic heirs, and found them full of wisdom, and though he had come to accept, in some sense, the truth of Christian teaching, yet, by his own account, he never really understood either until his conversion, when God's grace acted in his heart.

He tells us how one day he was reading in a garden, or orchard, with a friend. He had by this time come to reject the errors of the Manichees, to which he had been devoted for years, and had been brought by the wisdom of the works of Plato that he read, and by the holiness of the life of St Ambrose that he had witnessed, to some understanding of the Christian message. But the chains of ambition and sensuality, he tells us, were too strong, and he could not or would not submit his will and change his life to fit those teachings. Perhaps for him there was no difference between 'could not' and 'would not': perhaps there never is for a person in such a predicament. As he was musing, sorrowfully, over his wretched state, the book laid aside, he heard a voice from a neighbouring garden. It was a child's voice, chanting over and over again the words '*Tolle, lege*': take up and read. Augustine was aware that children in their play very often do chant words that have little or no meaning for themselves or for others: but, distracted and reflective as he was, he realised that not only were these words that he had never heard before in any child's play, but that they were words that had a direct meaning for him. He took up and read: he picked up his discarded book and opened it, and his eye fell on St Paul's exhortation to the Romans to live as befits children of light.

By his act of humility – that of taking the inconsequential babblings of a child's play as containing a message from God for himself, the intellectual – the spell that kept him chained in his wretchedness, the spell of sensuality and ambition, was broken. The words of St Paul, which he might well have read many times before, were for the first time effective in him. He had been touched by grace, and he believed: he was a new man.

The features of this conversion were to be the model upon which he was to understand his whole life – and, indeed, the whole of human life. It was not just a question of realising that mere understanding was insufficient to produce action, to draw down salvation: he could have read this in Plato and Aristotle. In different ways, this truth had been and was to be repeated a thousand times by philosophers, and Augustine's own life had given him ample evidence of it. Indeed, he had known it before his conversion: otherwise, why should he have been sorrowful as he sat in the orchard? What his conversion made him realise was that without grace, without the attitude of humility, of being willing to listen even to a child's babbling as if it were an oracle from God, there was no possibility of real understanding at all. It is likely that he had read the passage from St Paul already: but, even if not, its message, of the need for a new manner of life, had been taught him in a thousand ways, and had been all too obvious to him for years. His problem had been that he *had not wanted* a new manner of life. The humility of listening to the child's voice, the faith that God gave him in that moment of opening the book, were decisive: he could now understand the text of St Paul because now – by a secret miracle that God could work in any heart – that text could become part of his life.

All this explains why we find in Augustine's writings what to us is a paradoxical claim: that reason follows on from faith. 'Authority', he insists, 'demands faith of us, and prepares man for reason'. This claim appears paradoxical not only to the average modern person, but even to those among us who share or who claim to share Augustine's own faith. For it seems to be a teaching of that faith that 'grace supposes nature': that God gives us his divine gifts in a definite order. First we are given life, and then grace: life is given to all, grace only to some. This teaching does not suppose that there are limits on God's generosity: God can give his gifts as and when he pleases. But it does seem to be a fact that he prefers to give them in this order. In vivid terms, you have to make a baby before you can christen it. Parenthood is seen by Christian faith as a sharing in God's creative power, and thus no less a gift of God than his making of the infant a child of God's favour at its christening. But the order is there: first God's gift through nature, i.e. parenthood and birth; then God's gift through grace, i.e. becoming a child of God.

An application of this doctrine can be made in the field of faith and reason, and it seems directly contrary to Augustine's view. Reason is a gift that God makes to the whole human race, while the Christian faith, though perhaps in some sense offered to all, is taken up only by a few: indeed, perhaps it can be taken up only by a few. Christian teachers are therefore expected to struggle to remove by the exercise of reason the weeds of ordinary human error in their pupils before they can hope that the seed of faith will take root.

Besides being a matter of Christian tradition, this view seems a matter of common sense. We should not see Augustine, then, as plainly disagreeing with it. What he wishes to do is to insist that as a matter of fact, in his own life and, he thinks, in the lives of others too, it is only when enlightened by Christian faith that the reason can reach its full stature. Grace does indeed suppose nature, and faith supposes reason. But grace elevates nature, and faith corrects and improves reason. It was only after his moment of conversion that Augustine could understand and make his own the clear words of St Paul. Still more strikingly, he found that it was only after his conversion that he could understand even what Plato had said. To Augustine the Christian, new meanings were revealed in the writings of Plato. They could be read as pointing the way to

Christian faith, and that was their true meaning, the meaning which God had brought about through Plato, though Plato himself had not fully understood it.

So while Augustine would no doubt have agreed that the existence of the reason precedes the existence of faith, his position is that the full and true understanding that reason can give, the proper exercise of the reason, can only come once the Christian faith has been accepted. This acceptance can come about only through humility, through the action of the will in subjecting the reason to authority.

We can see here a special case of the notion of authority which was dealt with in Chapter 2. It is a special case, a supreme case, because the authority is that of God. But considered as a question of the attitudes of mind that a person takes up in accepting an authority, this supreme case does not differ intrinsically from any other case. It is only more striking from the circumstances in which it came about. Augustine, after all, was not sitting at the feet of an obviously wise master, which would be the normal case of accepting an authority. He was in fact attending to the babblings of a child. But though the words had no meaning for the child, they had a meaning for Augustine: because through the child, as Augustine came to realise. God was speaking.

4.2 FAITH AND REASON IN THE AUGUSTINIAN TRADITION

Augustine could easily have made his own the motto of St Anselm. St Anselm, a thinker in the Augustinian tradition many centuries later (1033–1109), took as the programme of his investigations the phrase '*Credo ut intelligam*': I believe in order that I may understand. For both Anselm and Augustine, it was impossible that understanding should precede faith. Augustine had tried that way and it had led him only to the sorrow in which he sat in the orchard. That kind of understanding led nowhere: it was not, indeed, true understanding at all.

Once faith had been given, understanding might follow: and, in fact, one of the tasks into which the converted Augustine threw himself was that of developing that understanding. He now had in his hand, he thought, the thread with which he could find a path through the labyrinth of secular learning. All his own learning – great as it was – could be seen in a new perspective, as contributing to the understanding given by his faith, and thus valuable; or as failing to contribute, and thus worthless. He could look back on his schooldays and see what was good and bad in them, and sift the value of his early linguistic and literary studies. He could look back, too, at his later studies among the philosophers, and distinguish what was true in them, what could be used to contribute to the understanding of his faith from what had to be rejected. Everything in the world fitted into the understanding of his new-found Christian faith. The truths achieved by philosophers could be understood as consistent with the truths of faith, and thus helping to develop Augustine's understanding of his faith. The falsehoods of the philosophers could now be seen as false in the light of his faith, and could be rejected. The task which Augustine set himself he saw as one given by God: the Christian faith contained everything that was necessary for salvation, but it did not give a complete understanding of the world. As Augustine pointed out in one of his commentaries on Genesis, God's purpose in giving us the Scriptures was to make Christians of us, not mathematicians or astronomers. A corollary of this is that if we want to be mathematicians or astronomers as well as Christians, if we want to understand more of God's greatness as shown in the Creation, we have to make our own investigations.

This project of Augustine's went through various phases, the experts tell us: phases in which philosophical ideas, mostly drawn from the Neoplatonists, were more or less important in his thought. The project was not finished at his death: he would not have expected it to be. He knew that his faith was a gift from God, and that God is infinitely rich: hence Augustine himself, should God so choose, might continually receive more faith, and thus more possibilities of understanding. If faith could always increase, then the understanding that followed on faith, the use of reason to develop what could be known of the intellectual context of faith and to reject errors that went against it, was also capable of continual improvement. Augustine himself might have hoped that he would continue to be yet more enlightened by God, as by God's grace he increased in his likeness to God, after that first conversion. But he would also have held that those who came after him might be holier, and thus more enlightened by God. In any case, those who came after him would be able to develop their own understanding of the faith on the basis of Augustine's understanding. Future generations of believers would already have received, through Augustine's writings, the gifts that God had already made to Augustine.

We can see, then, how it was natural for Augustine's conception of wisdom and authority to give rise to a tradition. Understanding could develop, with faith, through the life of an individual who lived in obedience to God's authority, as Augustine had done after his conversion. It could also develop, in the same way, through the life of the Church as a whole. When Augustine died in 430 AD the civilisation he knew was crumbling – in fact, the northern barbarians were at that very time laying siege to Hippo, the Roman-African city in which he lived, and of which he was the last Catholic bishop. Nevertheless, the tradition that had its origins in him did live on, did develop, in spite of all the troubles of the centuries that followed. The motto from Anselm – I believe in order that I may understand – which centuries later was to sum up the Augustinian attitude to wisdom, shows that the tradition lived on. Anselm was born among the descendants of the Burgundian barbarians who had established themselves in the Alps, and worked among the descendants of the Scandinavian and Saxon barbarians who had established themselves in what Augustine had known as the further limits of the civilised world, at that time slowly being detached from civilisation and culture and given over to what appeared to be mere savage anarchy. Anselm's situation, then, was very different from Augustine's. Nevertheless, we can see in him a clear intellectual and spiritual descendant of the greatest of the Western Church Fathers.

The marks of the Augustinian tradition continued to be those which Augustine had set on it. Faith must come first, if real understanding is to be possible; but once faith has been given, the way is open for reason to work towards the development of a more perfect understanding. Any thesis put forward by any thinker can be dealt with either one way or another by the understanding that follows on faith: if the thesis is true, that understanding will recognise this, and find a way of incorporating it; while if the thesis is false, then that understanding will recognise its falsehood, and show it to be false. The notion of synthesis, of harmonisation and reconciliation, which was also stressed in chapter 2, is an essential part of the Augustinian tradition.

4.3 KEY CONCEPTS OF THE AUGUSTINIAN TRADITION

Given the origin of Augustine's own understanding, it is not surprising that the central concepts of that understanding – his philosophy – have to do with thought and life, and the relationship between them. This does not mean that he began with, or regarded as crucial, a 'theory of knowledge' in the sense in which we have become familiar with the notion since Descartes. The foundation of knowledge and wisdom for Augustine, as we have seen, was not some set of first principles that are available to all thinking beings, but the acceptance of God's authority, which is available only to those to whom God chooses to give it. That is why, when he asked himself what is the most important of virtues, he answered, memorably, in a way that would be incomprehensible to the pagan sages he so often relied on: the most important virtue is humility; and the second most important, humility; and the third most important, humility.

Yet it was not enough for Augustine to accept that God had taught him, and leave it at that: he took it to be his duty to find out how it was that God had taught him. The desire to understand, he had to suppose, was put into human beings by God, and should be followed up, once the human being realised that only by God and in God could that understanding be achieved.

Augustine was familiar with the problems associated with knowledge which had been introduced by Plato. For Plato, and for Augustine, an important and fascinating question was how it is possible for there to be unchanging and eternally true knowledge, such as mathematical knowledge, in human beings. It would seem that all our knowledge comes to us, as it does to the animals, through our senses: but how can our changeable senses give us knowledge of unchangeable mathematical truths, or of the ultimate reality of the natures of things? All that our senses can give us are sensations: an unintelligible mass of colours, shapes, sounds, textures, smells, tastes, and the like.

> But I hear that there are three kinds of inquiry: does it exist? what is it? and, of what sort is it? Now, I do indeed possess the images of the sounds of which these words are composed, and I know that they passed through the air as noise, and that they do not now exist any more. But as for the realities that are signified by these sounds! I never came in contact with *them* through my bodily senses. I never grasped them except with my mind. Nonetheless, in my memory are laid up not the images of these realities, but the very realities themselves. How did they get into me? Can they tell me? I run over all the entry-points of my body, but I cannot find which one they came in by. My eyes tell me 'If they were coloured, it was we who told you of them'. The ears say 'If they made a noise, it was we who drew them to your attention'. The nostrils say 'If they had an odour, they came in through us'. The sense of taste says 'If they had no savour, then do not ask me about them'. The sense of touch says 'If it was not a body, then I did not handle it; and if I did not handle it, it was not I who gave you news of it'. (*Confessions*, Book X Chapter 10)

Or then again, Augustine wonders, how is it that we can remember what is no longer present to our senses? And how is it that we can even remember having forgotten. Perhaps it is partly this question about memory that means that while Augustine accepts that Plato has rightly understood the problem, he cannot accept Plato's answer as it stands. Plato holds that in our knowledge of changeless truths we are in some way in contact with changeless realities – what he calls the Forms or Ideas. For Plato, the things that we see around us in the world are no more than likenesses of the true reality. For example, the many beautiful things in the world are just imperfect copies of the Beautiful, the many pairs of things we see around us are just likenesses of or sharers in the Two, and so on. Our minds are able to grasp this reality of the Forms which is outside the world. Augustine is able to accept most of this: but he cannot accept Plato's explanation of how it comes about. Plato tells us that when we think we are acquiring for the first time the concepts in terms of which our knowledge of changeless reality is expressed, we are in fact *remembering*: remembering a purely intellectual vision which our souls had in a previous existence. Since Plato identifies the soul and the person, he would in fact say not that our souls had this vision, but that we had it.

Augustine in some of his works seems to toy with this idea of recollection: but it has serious difficulties. The usual difficulty which is raised by commentators nowadays is that if, as Plato alleges, we cannot understand how we could acquire such knowledge in this life, it is surely even harder to understand how we could have acquired it in another. Augustine is more likely to have had other worries. First, there is his worry about memory: memory is at least as obscure and mysterious a reality as is our knowledge of mathematics or of the beautiful. Then, the notion of the pre-existence of souls hardly seems consistent with traditional Christian belief. Lastly, and perhaps most importantly, the identification which Plato makes between the soul and the person seems directly contrary to Christian belief in the resurrection of the body.

Augustine's own solution is to draw a parallel between human knowledge in general and what he knows of the special case of knowledge by faith, which, being given by God, is beyond the intellectual powers of any unaided human being. But once the knowledge of faith is granted it enables one to look back on all the previous strivings of the human mind, and to recognise them as either true or false. In a similar way, intellectual knowledge itself – the kind of knowledge that any human being may have – is beyond the powers of the unaided human senses, but confers intelligibility on the information or raw data that the senses produce. 'It is not the body that senses, but the soul through the body.' Thus Augustine in book ten of the *Confessions* concludes that all intellectual knowledge is, like faith, a divine illumination. He does this by taking up Plato's notion of the Forms or Ideas and making them into ideas in a more modern sense: ideas in the mind of God. They are originals, patterns, exemplars, which God makes use of in making the world. For Augustine, then, as for Plato, this world is just the copy of a truer reality, just as the reflection in a mirror is a copy of the truer reality of what is reflected. God also uses these exemplars to communicate knowledge to us: our own minds thus have some share in the knowledge of the divine mind, they contain likenesses of God's eternal ideas. That is how changeless knowledge can exist in the changing minds of animals like ourselves.

The notion that all knowledge, and not just faith, is a gift from God, becomes the hallmark of the Augustinian tradition. Hence, Anselm uses the fact that there exists a thought of God as the basis of an argument to convict of inconsistency the one who denies God's existence. The notion is seen, too, in the *Didascalion* of Hugo of St Victor which dates from the early part of the twelfth century (its author died in 1141 AD). There were the years in which the Paris schools came to their flourishing, not long before they amalgamated in the single entity of the University. The book is a discussion of how study and knowledge should be organised. Hugo clearly felt that in the development of the Augustinian tradition – a development which, as we have seen, is part of Augustine's original conception – some important features of Augustine's own thought were being lost from sight. He wrote his book to recall scholars to the need for faith and humility, and to a reliance on the light that only God could shine on them. He holds that the wisdom of God shows itself in two different kinds of work: in the work of creation and in the work of salvation. The writings of what we earlier called the secular canon deal with the former, the writings of Holy Scripture deal with the latter. It is Hugo's purpose to remind students that secular knowledge is valuable only in so far as it is enlightened by Christian faith and helps in the understanding of that faith. As he says at the start of his first chapter, 'Of all things, the first that should be sought is that wisdom in which the form of the perfect good stands fixed. Wisdom enlightens man so that he may recognise himself' – that is to say, recognise himself by recognising that he depends on God.

Another important feature of Augustine's thought is the notion that evil is a privation: it is not something positive, a sort of mirror-image of the goodness of God. That which is evil is evil only by the absence of some good. This idea was not original to

Augustine – he seems to have derived it from the great Neoplatonist Plotinus (c.204–270) – but it was Augustine who most insisted on it and made it part of western thought. The error of making evil a positive reality had been the chief feature of the beliefs of the Manichees, an eclectic religious group with Iranian origins, which was very widespread in Augustine's day, and of which he had been a believing member in earlier years. The doctrine that evil is a negation is therefore important for Augustine's own faith in one almighty and creative God. Obviously the doctrine has theological roots, but it has extremely wide-ranging consequences outside the field of theology. Once the concept existed that the opposite of a positive quality might not be a negative quality, but simply nothing, it became possible to stop thinking of the world, as the ancient Greeks had thought of it, as being the battle-ground of warring opposite qualities. (I owe this point, and much, much else, to Professor P.T. Geach.)

It is quite natural to believe that one thing is, say, hotter than another because its heat is mixed in with a lesser amount of cold. The doctrine that evil is a negation meant that this was not the only way of looking at things. From Augustine onwards it was impossible to believe that one thing was less good than another because its goodness was mixed in with a greater amount of evil. Goodness, so to speak, was a quality which could vary in intensity down to zero without for that reason turning into its opposite or becoming mixed up with its opposite.

Once it was realised that this was true with regard to goodness, it could only be a step to wondering whether it was not true of other qualities. The concept of intensive magnitude, which has made modern science possible, had been born. It is true that this concept was applied to the physical world only little by little. For a long time, and for the most part, at the more popular level, medieval people were happy to believe that the world and the human body were made up out of elements or humours which were characterised by pairs of opposing qualities: earth and black bile were dry and cold, air and blood were wet and hot, fire and red bile were dry and hot, water and phlegm were wet and cold. This fragment of archaic science is one of the best-known features of popular medieval beliefs. But this archaic chemistry and physiology did not block all possibilities of development, as the theoretical concepts on which they were based had for the Greeks. The concept of intensive magnitude was in the end to triumph, in the work of the great sixteenth- and seventeenth-century physicists, after its use and development by medieval philosophers.

4.4 A PARALLEL DEVELOPMENT IN THE EAST

Towards the latter end of the fifth century, the century in which Augustine died, there lived another thinker, probably in a monastery in Syria, whose name is unknown to us. His works bear the pseudonym of 'Dionysius the Areopagite', that is, they are written in the name of a member of the religious council of Athens who had been converted by St Paul in the first century. Readers in the Middle Ages took this pseudonym seriously, and treated these works with the respect due to those of a great thinker of the past who had been brought up amid the highest pagan wisdom, and had heard the teaching of St Paul himself. We now know that this attribution is a mistake: but the works of Pseudo-Dionysius, as we now call him, are well worthy of respect, even if they have turned out to be four hundred years more recent than medieval scholars thought them to be.

Pseudo-Dionysius is in many ways like Augustine – a Christian deeply impressed by a Christian understanding of the works of Plato and the Neoplatonists, who attempts to make a synthesis. We have seen how for the Saint all the teachings of human wisdom could be definitively incorporated into the understanding that comes from faith, or definitively rejected. When reading Pseudo-Dionysius one sometimes feels that he should have done a little more rejecting and a little less incorporating. For example, the way he relates the One of the Neoplatonists – the supreme intelligible reality, beyond even the Ideas or Forms – with the Christian God seems to give away too much Christian faith and keep too much neo-Platonism. But despite the fact that there is room to disagree with some of his teachings, and despite the fact that Augustine probably would have disagreed, Pseudo-Dionysius seem to be involved in the same kind of project. Certainly, one of his most important doctrines, just mentioned in connection with Augustine, is that evil is a privation. Linked with this is a doctrine continually cited during the Middle Ages, that good and evil are not symmetrical. 'Good is caused by an integrity of factors, evil by any single defect': that is, a thing can be good only if everything about it is good, but it is bad if only one thing about it is bad.

The most influential doctrine which Pseudo-Dionysius gives us concerns how it is possible to talk about God. God is quite unlike us, and quite unlike anything in our experience: but our language has been developed to deal with our experience. How, then, is it possible for us to use that language to say anything true and intelligible about God?

We can talk about God, Pseudo-Dionysius tells us, in two ways: by denying and by affirming. We can, and should, deny of God any imperfection or limitation that we find in the world. Hence we must say that God is not changeable, does not die, is not subject to limitations, as creatures are. On the other hand, we should also affirm of God, in a super-eminent way, all the perfections that can be found in the world which are compatible with the fact that God is not subject to any limitation. To be wise and to be powerful are perfections in the world, and they do not of themselves imply any limitation: so we can affirm that God is superlatively wise and superlatively powerful. We could not say, though, that God is superlatively big, because although size is in some sense a perfection in the world, it implies the limitation of being a physical body: so this perfection cannot be affirmed of God.

This doctrine, like the doctrine that evil is a privation, has applications far outside the theological context in which it has its origin: it provided medieval thinkers with an understanding of the notion of analogy. The notion of analogy is, roughly speaking, the notion that an expression can be used with slightly differing senses without becoming hopelessly ambiguous. When we use the same words of God and of human beings – when, to use a medieval example, we say that God is wise and Socrates is wise – we cannot be using the word 'wise' in exactly the same sense in both halves of the sentence. But the two senses are not for that reason entirely different: if they were, if the word 'wise' in these two contexts were simply ambiguous as the English word 'staff' is, then it would tell us nothing to say that God is wise. As it is, the two senses are not identical, but they have a systematic connection which can be investigated. It was this investigation which was to prove so philosophically fruitful when it was linked up with Aristotle's teachings on the different but connected senses of words such as 'existent', 'true' and 'good'.

4.5 PROBLEMS FOR THE AUGUSTINIAN APPROACH

The great aim of Augustine and his heirs, as we have said, was to reach understanding through faith. Once the faith was received from God, understanding and true reasoning could follow: the world and God could be understood, by the exercise of reason in the light of the Christian faith. Every teaching of human wisdom could either be seen to be true and incorporated into this understanding, or be seen to be false and be rejected. The question is, though, how could falsehoods be rejected? It was the answers to this question that provided a danger for the tradition that stemmed from Augustine.

Take, for example, the belief of the pagan philosophers, including Plato, that the heavenly bodies are in some way divine. This is false, Christian (and Jewish and Muslim) faith tells us: this, then, is part of the teaching of the philosophers which cannot be incorporated into a Christian understanding of the world. It must be rejected: but on what grounds? Must it be rejected solely on the basis of the authority of faith, or could the Augustinian thinker find flaws in the arguments which led the pagan philosophers to this false conclusion?

It is perhaps not easy to know what answer Augustine himself would have given to the general problem. (Though certainly in the particular case he gives absolutely conclusive counter-examples and counter-arguments to the notion that the planets, as superior beings, influence the course of human lives.) Partly the answer may depend on how clever the individual Augustinian thinker is, and how clever the pagan philosophers were. The Augustinian thinker, having the Christian faith, is wiser, but he may not be so clever, and thus may not in fact be able to refute the false arguments which the clever pagan philosophers have put forward. But in reacting to this, which may appear a mere practical difficulty, a fateful difference of approach may arise.

Some Augustinian thinkers might hold that there must always be a way to refute the errors of the pagans, without appealing to the content of Christian faith. After all, such a thinker might say, we know by faith that the conclusion is false, so we know that the arguments by which those conclusions are reached must be erroneous. Hence such thinkers will believe that there exists a purely rational refutation of the false view without appealing to the content of the Christian faith, even if they discover that they are not clever enough to find it out.

But there is another possible attitude, which can also find support in Augustine. This attitude might lead people to say that perhaps the human mind, even enlightened by God, is so weak and so distorted by human vices, that it simply cannot find any refutation of the errors of the pagan philosophers – or of Christian heretics, for that matter. It is only by God's special gift of faith that the error can be seen as the falsehood that it is: we need not expect a further gift which will show us in exactly what way the error is an error. After all, such a person might say, true understanding can come only after faith. We should not, then, be surprised when we find a lack of true understanding apart from the faith. And we should certainly not expect that an understanding which does not include faith will be able to solve all problems and refute all errors.

Thus there was always a danger among thinkers in the Augustinian tradition of falling into the attitude of mind that is called fideism, an attitude of despairing of the powers of the human mind, except when they are specially aided by faith. This, in the end, could lead to the breakdown of the Augustinian project of incorporating all human wisdom into the understanding that follows on faith. For if, as fideists think, we may at any time come up against ineradicable errors in the exercise of reason – if, as they believe, faith alone can guarantee truth – then sooner or later a very large proportion of the teachings of merely human reason is going to be seen as irrelevant to the faith, and as irreconcilable with it. The fideist cannot incorporate these teachings, because they are not true; but he cannot, either, see what partial truths there may be in them, which he could incorporate, because he cannot identify which elements led to the erroneous conclusion. Such a thinker is content with rejecting all these teachings in the name of his faith, and he no longer cares to argue about why they should be rejected. Thus great fields of thought will be left alone, to their own devices, beyond the reach of the Augustinian project. And this usually means that these fields of thought will be left to those who do not share Augustine's faith: pagans, Jews, Muslims, heretics, or straightforward infidels.

There is equally a danger, with fideism, that the understanding that has already been achieved within the tradition will become fossilized. Some elements of human wisdom have been incorporated – by Augustine himself, let us say – into the understanding that the tradition hands down, because these elements fit with the faith and can be used to help in understanding it. The temptation for the fideist will be to attribute to these incorporated human teachings the firmness of divine faith, since they have come to form part of a Christian understanding based on faith, and to refuse to look at rival teachings that perhaps might be used to develop understanding yet further. This is to attribute to a merely human authority, the authority of Augustine, say, the force that belongs only to divine authority. It is to refuse to admit the point which was made in chapter 2, that while an argument from human authority is indeed an argument, it is the weakest of all arguments.

The Augustinian tradition, then, runs the risk of becoming fideistic, of stagnating, of becoming dogmatic in the bad sense. It runs the risk, in the end, of frustrating its own capability to achieve its own project. That project is to incorporate all human wisdom into the understanding that arises from faith: to fall into fideism is, in practice, to abandon that project.

5

AN ALTERNATIVE
TENDENCY

5.1 A METHODOLOGICAL DISTINCTION
BETWEEN FAITH AND REASON

The claim that the argument from human authority is the weakest of all arguments comes originally, as we saw, from Boethius (c.480–524). Though Boethius is roughly a contemporary of Pseudo-Dionysius, he seems, as the quotation reveals, to have a rather different attitude to human wisdom from that shown by the authors touched on in the last chapter. Augustine, as we have seen, insists on the impossibility of understanding without faith. Boethius prefers to make some kind of a distinction between the realms of faith and reason, at least in some of his works, if not in his life. Another author, more or less contemporary with Augustine (i.e. late fourth to early fifth centuries) who shows a tendency similar to that of Boethius is Chalcidius. And it is possible to find such a distinction being made by other authors who follow them, throughout the Middle Ages.

It seems that both Boethius and Chalcidius are strongly impressed by the notion that each science – each discipline of knowledge – has its own methods and subject-matter. Boethius devotes an interesting discussion to this theme – which appears to have originated in Aristotle – at the start of one of his theological works, the *De*

74

Trinitate. Boethius is clearly very familiar with at least some of Aristotle's work, and he has a great admiration for it. Chalcidius is more of a Platonist – he is known only through his commentary in Latin on Plato's dialogue, the *Timaeus*. But by the time of Chalcidius Aristotle's logic and theory of science had largely been adopted by the Neoplatonists, the most influential philosophical school of the time, as a result of the work of Porphyry (c.232–c.304). This pupil of Plotinus (c.204–270), saw Aristotelian logic as an excellent tool for the development of his master's neo-Platonic metaphysics.

Once one holds the idea that each science has its own proper subject-matter and methodology, it becomes possible to make a distinction between reason and faith which is quite different from the Augustinian attitude. Both Boethius and Chalcidius, in contrast to Augustine, seem to have thought that there was a legitimate sphere for philosophical discussion which was not explicitly directed by Christian faith. To put it crudely, instead of using reason only to work forwards, to develop the understanding based on faith, they wanted to use reason to work backwards as well. They had the faith, and the understanding that came from it: they wanted to try to develop reason to the highest pitch it could reach before the illumination of faith. No doubt, as faithful believers, they wanted their conclusions to be consistent with the faith (as in fact they were), and they would have been willing to hold the conclusions they reached by the use of their reason tentatively, to say the least, if there even appeared to be a conflict with the faith: but the point is that they strictly excluded from their philosophical works considerations drawn from truths known only because of God's direct revelation. This is the hall-mark of their writings, and of the tendency in medieval thought that arises from them.

This methodological exclusion of faith from philosophical consideration is so marked that at times it has been doubted whether Chalcidius was a Christian at all; and it was even suggested at one time that Boethius the philosopher and Boethius the theologian were two different authors. This last suggestion has been proved false: but there still may be people who hold that Boethius may have abandoned his faith in the last, difficult months of his life, as he lay in prison, awaiting execution for alleged complicity in a conspiracy against King Theoderic. But this suggestion lacks evidence, and does not seem reasonable: it is rather the the reaction of fideism. We know that Boethius believed in a methodological distinction between faith and reason, and between philosophy and theology, so there is no reason to suppose that he did not die as he had lived, as a Christian. The fact that his last work, composed in prison, is a philosophical work and does not contain the name of Christ, is not the least evidence to the contrary. It is perhaps worth mentioning that Boethius was, and perhaps still is, venerated as a martyr in the place where he died: this is evidence of what those who witnessed his last years thought of him.

There is nothing in Boethius that is inconsistent with the faith. Nor is there any such inconsistency in Chalcidius which cannot be explained away as merely an exposition of Plato's opinions. On the face of it, there is at least as much unorthodoxy in the work of Pseudo-Dionysius, who is undoubtedly a Christian and only seldom suspected even of the slightest deliberate heresy. The difference between the writings of Boethius and Chalcidius, on the one hand, and those of Augustine and Pseudo-Dionysius on the other, seems very clearly to be a difference of approach more than anything else. However, such a difference may still be an important one. The approach of Boethius and Chalcidius faces problems no less than those faced by that of Augustine, though of an opposite kind.

5.2 KEY CONCEPTS IN BOETHIUS AND CHALCIDIUS

The philosophical task which Boethius set himself was that of translating Aristotle into Latin, and so introducing him to the West. He then intended to effect a reconciliation, a synthesis, between Plato and Aristotle. The synthesis was never really begun – Boethius was a busy statesman as well as a scholar – but the introduction of at least some key notions of Aristotle's logic, and of some of the metaphysics on which they rested, was undoubtedly a success.

We have already mentioned that the Neoplatonists, particularly Porphyry, had adopted Aristotle's logic as the best tool they could find to develop their master's theories. Porphyry (c.232–c.304) was a pupil of Plotinus, whose works he helped to edit. He thought that the logic of Aristotle could be separated from its metaphysical context and used as a valuable tool in the development of Neoplatonic metaphysics. He wrote an introduction to Aristotle's logic, the *Isagoge*, which was also translated by Boethius.

Basic concepts of Aristotle's logic, with some of their metaphysical background, were thus part of the common coin of intellectual discourse in the East: and, more importantly, they had been incorporated into Christian teaching in order to clarify the faith in the great controversies between the orthodox and the innovators over the teachings about the Trinity and about Christ. It was the achievement of Boethius to make these common notions easily available in the West, where knowledge of Greek was dwindling. Boethius's Aristotelian tendencies also gave him an interest in producing definitions, some of which – for example, the definitions of 'person' and of 'eternity' – are still in philosophical use today and look like continuing to be so.

The key Aristotelian concepts that Boethius introduced into the West are those which are found in Aristotle's *Categories*: particularly the notion of substance, and related notions. The word 'substance' is in its origins apparently ambiguous, and even when developed by Aristotle it appears to stand for a group of related concepts rather than for a single one. If we are looking for an equivalent term in modern philosophical discourse, which, while going some way to explain what Aristotle was about, would avoid the associations which have grown up as part of Aristotelian or post-Aristotelian theory, perhaps the best choice would be 'entity'. (This suggestion is made by Professor G.E.M. Anscombe in her essay 'Aristotle' in Anscombe and Geach, 1961.) The metaphysics which underpins Aristotle's logic is by and large an effort to determine what are the basic entities of which the world consists. This effort – as Aristotle very well knew – had previously been made by the pre-Socratic philosophers and by Plato, though their approaches and answers had been very different.

The problem that these earlier thinkers had found most puzzling, according to Aristotle's own account, was that of change. It seems obvious that many things in the world around us are in process of change: but if this is so, what is it that is changing? Something that is changing is neither what it used to be nor what it is turning into, by definition. Nor is it anything definite while it is changing: if it were, then it would be that definite thing, and therefore not, after all, in process of change. But how can a thing exist without being a definite something? And even if it does exist – which seems impossible – how can we say anything true about it? Anything we say about it will attribute to it something definite, since our language consists of expressions with definite and fixed meanings. So if the thing is changing, attributing something definite to it will be a falsehood.

This puzzle gave rise to various answers. One was that of Parmenides. According to Parmenides, apparently, we know that something exists, and that nothing can exist without being definite. We also know that if something changes it cannot be anything definite. Parmenides is forced to conclude, then, that nothing changes: change, and indeed multiplicity, must be illusions that we suffer from.

Another view, quite the opposite of this one, is often attributed to Heraclitus. The experts now tell us that this attribution is probably mistaken: but the view can perhaps be truly attributed to Heraclitus's radical disciple Cratylus. According to this view, we know that change exists, and, indeed, that many things which appear to be changeless are in fact in process of change. Since this is so, then nothing is anything definite, and therefore nothing can really exist at all – or, at least, if anything does exist, it is impossible for us to say anything true about it. Aristotle records that Cratylus himself held this view so strongly and consistently that in the end he gave up even trying to say anything, and would just move his finger. Aristotle, alas, does not record *how* Cratylus moved his finger.

A more interesting view is the one that the experts now tell us that Heraclitus himself probably held. Heraclitus says, in one of his epigrams 'On those who step down into the same rivers, other and other waters forever flow'. Thus what is describable as *the same river*, and indeed describable in a definite way as the same river, is not describable as and is not *the same water*. The element of continuity in the continual flux of change Heraclitus calls *logos*, literally 'word' or 'expression'. Perhaps 'description' is a suitably vague translation, but no single English word can convey the connotations that *logos* may have had for him.

Two lines of thoughts stem from these debates. One is the line of those called by Aristotle 'the physicists'. They tried to maintain that everything that exists and changes is really, fundamentally, one thing, one kind of stuff, or a mixture of a very few kinds of stuff – typically earth, air, fire and water. These 'elements' would thus be the only entities, the only things that really exist: everything else would be nothing more than manifestations of the ways in which these basic entities affect one another.

The other line of thought is that of Plato. He was impressed, as Augustine was to be later, by the fixity and immutability of knowledge. How was this possible in the changing world? His answer, as we have mentioned, was that apart from the changing world that we see there are other entities which are not subject to any change, not even the change involved in combining with others of the same kind. These are the Forms or Ideas: things in this changing world are imperfect resemblances of these, or sharers in some way in their being. This is the notion which Augustine takes up and turns into that of the ideas or exemplars in the mind of God according to which the world is made, and by sharing in which our imperfect, changeable and mortal minds are made capable of sharing in eternal truths. These, for Plato, are the only real entities.

When Aristotle enters the debate he refuses to side either with the 'physicists' or with his master Plato. For Aristotle, the basic entities – the 'substances' – are what we generally take them to be, the individual things we see around us: people, plants, animals, rocks. These can change, of course, and cease to exist, but while they exist they are something definite enough for us to be able to speak truly about them. They are not, as the physicists would have it, mere combinations and relations of the elements, which would be for them the only real entities. Nor are they, as Plato thought, just copies or reflections of the real entities, the Ideas or Forms. No, the individual things we see around us are real entities; and he adopts the word 'entity', the word usually translated 'substance', to mean these things.

It is necessary for Aristotle to distinguish between these substances and other existents or entities which are not so basic. A substance, such as a cat, is not to be identified with its size, shape, or weight, since obviously it can and does change in any or all of these respects without ceasing to exist, without ceasing to be itself, without ceasing to be one and the same cat. These other entities – the qualities or determinations of the cat, we might say – are not *what the cat is* but are things that *are in* the cat, to use Aristotle's expression. By the time of Boethius, these other, non-substantial, non-basic kinds or 'categories' of existent had come to be called 'accidents' of the cat: literally, 'things that happen' to the cat.

This distinction is one that we perhaps very naturally make. But there is still a question about whether Aristotle is right in his identification of substances. Are the things he picks out as substances really substances, basic existents? The distinction he makes between substances and accidents would remain a valid one even if we were to claim, with the so-called physicists, that the only real substances are the elements. If this were so, then everything else – cats, people, rocks – would be no more than accidental determinations or combinations of these elementary substances, just as, for Aristotle, a football team or a pack of wolves is an accidental determination or combination of the individual animal substances that go to make it up.

Aristotle's distinction between substance and accident also remains valid even if we claim, with Plato and his school, that only the Forms are substances. If this were so, then what Aristotle takes to be a substance – this cat, say – is just an accidental likeness of the true Cat. Aristotle himself would not hold that the reflection of a cat in a mirror, or a picture of a cat, were substances, let alone real cats: and so the Platonists do not have to hold that this ordinary cat is a substance. It would be for them no more than an accidental reflection of the Form of Cat. It is for this reason that the Neoplatonists saw no difficulty in taking over Aristotle's terminology and the logic that went with it, while rejecting the metaphysical answers Aristotle offered about exactly what things were substances.

Aristotle had thus to give a more developed account of what it is to be a substance. The details of this can be left to the next chapter: here we need draw attention only to the logical and scientific structure that Aristotle uses to classify substances, in his preparation for giving a fuller account.

Substances are the most basic things that exist: they are also, for that reason, the most basic things that we talk about. Of the things that we say about a substance, some express what that substance is; others express what the accidents are that are in the substance. If we speak of the cat Ludo, we can say, perhaps, 'Ludo is a cat' or 'Ludo is black and white'. The name 'Ludo' in both sentences stands for this cat, this substance; the question is, what do the other parts of either sentence stand for?

In 'Ludo is a cat', according to Aristotle, the word 'cat' stands for what Ludo is. There is some slight confusion in Aristotle's terminology here. He uses the word 'substance' to mean 'what a name like "Ludo" stands for', and also to mean 'what a word like "cat" stands for'. That is, he uses the same word, 'substance', to mean an individual such as Ludo, and for the kind to which Ludo belongs, for what Ludo is. He does sometimes distinguish the two by calling what a name like 'Ludo' stands for 'first substance' and what a word like 'cat' stands for 'second substance', but all too often he fails to distinguish them, though context usually makes it clear which he means.

In the Middle Ages, and, I think, since then, partly as a result of Boethius's work, the word 'substance' tended to be used to mean what Aristotle sometimes called 'second substance', that is to say, the sort of thing a word like 'cat' stands for. When there was a danger of confusion, the terminology might be clarified by using the expression 'individual substance' for what Aristotle had sometimes called 'first substance', the particular individual a name like 'Ludo' stands for. Sometimes, too, the word 'hypostasis', transliterated from one of several Greek words meaning 'subject', was used to mean 'individual substance'. In some contexts the word 'person' also came to be used, and was memorably defined by Boethius as an individual substance of rational nature; that is, an individual substance that belongs to a kind of substance that is rational: e.g. an individual human being or angel.

The words 'nature' (as in the definition of 'person' just cited) and 'essence' were also used to help make these distinctions. The nature and essence of Ludo are that in virtue of which Ludo is a substance of the kind that he is, that is, that in virtue of which Ludo is a cat and can carry out typically feline activities. Meanwhile, the word 'subject', which Aristotle himself often used in a similar way to 'substance', came to be restricted more and more to the logical or grammatical meaning of 'subject of predication': what is being talked about in a sentence.

On the side of the accidents, as opposed to that of substance, there seems to have been the same kind of confusion in terminology: but it seems to have been judged less important to search out new terminology to avoid it. The word 'accident' is itself a coining after Aristotle's time, but it continued to be used to express two different notions. 'This accident' or 'this colour', say, could be used to mean the individual blackness or whiteness of Ludo, which would have a place and a time; but it could also be used to mean the kinds to which these individual colours belong: this kind of blackness, this kind of whiteness, which could equally well be found on another cat, in a photograph, or on a dog.

The kinds to which entities belong can be classified and related. every substance is a substance of a definite kind, as we have seen: Ludo is a cat, I am a human being. But both Ludo and I are animals: there is a higher kind to which the two kinds to which we belong themselves belong. The technical words used in this context are 'species' for the kinds that individual substances belong to, the kinds that tell us what those individuals are, and 'genus' (plural 'genera') for the kinds that these kinds in turn belong to. Thus 'cat' or 'human being' means a species, 'animal' means a genus.

But the adaptation, translation and introduction into the Latin West of Aristotle's logic was not the only achievement of Boethius which was influential in the Middle Ages. Another important discussion was his treatment of the notion of God's eternity, particularly in relation to problems caused by considerations related to human free will and divine foreknowledge. This, too, is in origin an Aristotelian problem. Aristotle wonders whether sentences about events in the future that may or may not happen are already true or false, or whether they only become true when the event they describe occurs. Either answer appears to be unsatisfactory. On the one hand it is unsatisfactory to say that 'It will rain tomorrow' is not yet true even if as a matter of fact it is going to rain tomorrow; but on the other hand it is equally unsatisfactory to say that 'It will rain tomorrow' is already true, since this seems to rule out the obvious possibility that it will not rain tomorrow.

The problem is heightened for a writer like Boethius since for him human actions must be contingent, non-necessary, undetermined, because they are free. On the other hand, Boethius cannot imagine that God is ignorant of how we will act, as if we could take God by surprise, or as if God had to wait and see what we get up to. This problem had a perennial interest at all kinds of levels in the Middle Ages, and elements taken from the discussions of Boethius appear in all kinds of contexts. (I seem to recall the cock and the hen in the Nun's Priest's tale in Chaucer's *Canterbury Tales* discussing the question, which would seem to make it a near-universal topic of discussion.)

Boethius tries two ways out of the dilemma. The first is to suggest that sentences about contingent events in the future may be true, but not 'definitely' true. It is necessarily true that either it will rain tomorrow or it will not rain tomorrow, but Boethius holds that it does not therefore follow that either it will necessarily rain tomorrow or it will necessarily not rain tomorrow. If it is true that it will rain tomorrow, then it is contingently true.

The other way out, which relates more specifically to God's knowledge, is to develop a famous metaphor that was frequently used by many different authors throughout the medieval period (and afterwards). God is eternal, and thus outside the succession of temporal events. He can thus survey that succession from the outside, just as someone standing in a high place might look down at a procession of travellers. The watcher on the hill-top sees what is happening below, but does not make it happen. In the same way, God knows how I will act tomorrow, but does not make me act. The application of this last point to God is one of the more doubtful aspects of the discussion since, of course, everything that happens in the world is in fact brought about by God, one way or another. Still, the metaphor is an important one philosophically, as well as historically.

The work of Chalcidius is rather different from that of Boethius: for a start it is rather more limited. It consists of a commentary in Latin on part of Plato's dialogue the *Timaeus*. This dialogue thus became the only dialogue of Plato that was at all known during the earlier Middle Ages in those parts of Europe where Latin rather than Greek had become the language of learning. The *Meno* and the *Phaedo* were also translated in the twelfth century, but they never came to rival the *Timaeus* in influence. This work is to modern eyes a curious and untypical dialogue. In it Plato abandons his usual concern with ethics and the theory of knowledge and speculates on the structure and origins of the world. It is an obscure work, but it could be, and by Chalcidius was, interpreted in a way that made it fairly consistent with Christian ideas about the Creation. This reading of the work gave a great deal of support to the attempt to show how far reason could reach, unaided by faith, in the understanding of the world.

5.3 PROBLEMS OF THE BOETHIAN APPROACH

We have said that the Augustinian approach ran the risk of falling into fideism: a use of the appeal to faith on every occasion. As a result it might find itself unable to take on new insights provided by the reflections of thinkers through the ages, and come to invest with an intangible sanctity the reflections of those who had already been admitted into the traditional understanding. The more Aristotelian approach of people like Boethius and Chalcidius runs the opposite risk of falling into a certain amount of rationalism. The teachings of the Christian faith are not explicitly referred to in the philosophical writings of thinkers in this line. Thus, even if these writings contain matters that go against the faith, this may be left uncorrected.

Of course, someone of the moral stature and consistency of life of Boethius, would even when translating or commenting on Aristotle, be very well aware of his own faith, and would not consciously allow whatever went against the faith to remain in his work. But what would happen in the case of a writer of a little less moral stature, a little less intelligent, a little more ambitious and a little more sure of himself?

Just as there is a danger in the Augustinian approach when it is taken by one less intellectually gifted than Augustine or Anselm, so there is danger in a Boethian approach when it is taken by one less strong in his Christian faith than Boethius himself. The danger in such a case is that the writer will take his own theories to be the truth: the ultimate truth that can be reached by the human mind unenlightened by faith. This sets up a tension: how can the highest achievements of the human mind – which is, after all, created by God – be inconsistent with what God teaches? This tension should lead the writer to revise his own theories; but it may very well lead him to adapt his view of the faith to fit the theories. This could be called a kind of rationalism: the medieval thinkers called it heresy. Either way, it was destructive of the medieval intellectual project.

Even if such attitudes did not lead directly to error and heresy, they would at least lead to a certain amount of separation between philosophy and theology, between faith and reason. We saw that the fideism into which the Augustinian approach can fall may lead to the same result. Hence a key to understanding the philosophical thought of the Middle Ages is to notice the fact of a tension between, on the one hand, these tendencies in each approach to separate faith from reason, and on the other, the desire which is present in both approaches to achieve a synthesis of all wisdom, both human and divine.

In the glance we took in the last chapter at the development of the Augustinian tradition, we skipped several centuries to look at the figures of St Anselm in the eleventh century and Hugo of St Victor in the twelfth. We can make such a leap on the side of the Aristotelian-Boethian approach, too. The centuries between the death of Boethius and the eleventh century were indeed dark ages, as far as philosophy was concerned. Not entirely, of course: there continued to be a handing down of tradition, and even some development, though more especially connected with theology. We have seen how Aquinas in the thirteenth century frequently cites the eighth century's John Damascene, who was responsible for handing on a good deal of Aristotelian moral teaching, and for developing the concept of the will. But the only figure in this dark period who seems to merit a chapter of his own in the usual accounts of medieval thought is the shadowy figure of John Scotus Eriugena, John the Scot of Ireland (c. 810–c.875).

This man was a Christian neo-Platonist in the manner of Pseudo-Dionysius, whom he translated into Latin. Like Pseudo-Dionysius, some of his expressions seem hardly consistent with Christian orthodoxy. Perhaps because of this, his own writings appear to have had little influence during the Middle Ages, though his translation of Pseudo-Dionysius was widely read. He is perhaps of more historical than philosophical significance: it is significant that at a time of widespread political disorder, and the degeneration of learning which tends to accompany disorder, there should be a profound and subtle – indeed, sometimes incomprehensibly subtle – scholar working away on the Neoplatonists in the remoteness of a far western island.

We can thus jump through to the eleventh century, and find there a startling illustration of the tensions that the different approaches in the tradition of learning could set up. In this period a fierce debate arose about the proper interpretation of the Aristotelian logical notions that had come down from Boethius.

It is not surprising that a renewal of philosophy should begin with logical problems: this is quite a common feature in the history of philosophy. In this case it took the form of raising the question of what degree of reality was possessed by genera and species, by what is signified by a general or universal expression like 'cat' which is true of all cats indifferently. This came to be called 'the problem of the universals'. Were genera and species constructions of the mind, imposed on all the differing individuals which we see in reality? Or were they in some sense more real than the individuals that we see? – a Platonic sort of answer. Or was the correct answer somewhere between the two? Did the genera and species exist in one way – divided up, as it were – in the individuals in the world, but in another, unified way, as single concepts in the mind?

In the first period of the debate thinkers seem to have inclined to the second position, the Platonic view which is technically known as 'extreme realism', since it attributes absolute reality to the universals. Anselm is sometimes said to have held this view, though it is debatable. He opposed a logician called Roscelin (c. 1050–

1120) who held the first view, commonly called 'nominalism', from the fact that it claims that e.g. all that cats have in common is that we call them all by the same name, 'cat'. By the turn of the twelfth century the chief upholder of extreme realism was one William of Champaux, who taught in the cathedral school in Paris. He was opposed in the name of the third position, known as 'moderate realism', by Abelard.

Abelard (1079–1142) was a man of great intelligence and force of character: he seems to have been dearly loved and greatly hated. Though he wished, no doubt, to reconcile divine and human wisdom, his was not the temperament that is naturally made for any kind of reconciliation. His logical work was outstanding, but, as a man of genius, he was naturally not content with this achievement. He saw it as his task to carry the new logical (and Aristotelian) insights that had been achieved by his victories in debates about the problem of universals into the field of reflection on the content of Christian faith and Christian morals. There can be, I think, no doubt that his conclusions in theology were unorthodox, to say the least: and he was rebuked by St Bernard both for unorthodoxy and for pride. St Bernard was no mean theologian himself, but he owed (and owes) his position to the reform and renewal of monastic life which he was carrying out and which survives to this day. It is also fair to say that he was a man of almost as difficult a temperament as Abelard. What makes Abelard a great man (as well as St Bernard), and what points out the difference between his day and our own, is that despite his own genius (which was probably superior to Bernard's) and despite his own confidence (which was at least equal to Bernard's) he accepted the rebuke. He submitted his work to the judgement of the Church, to those with authority, abandoning his own conclusions when authority judged them to be erroneous. As he himself said, he did not wish to be with Aristotle if it meant being separated from Christ.

It is important to realise that this submission was not, as it would be represented nowadays, a surrender of the rights of the truth and of free inquiry to the exercise of tyrannical authority. Abelard saw it as the surrender of a great mind to the paramount rights of the truth. Lesser men than Abelard might have hedged and temporised, might have in the first place avoided putting their speculations in so bold a form, and might have managed to keep their philosophy separate from their faith. Abelard, though, was committed to the project of synthesis; and though he may have failed in carrying out his part of the task, in his own eyes as well as in those of St Bernard and others, he succeeded in establishing the limits of permissible and legitimate development of the intellectual tradition. He established these limits first by overstepping them, and then, above all, by stepping back.

5.4 THE COEXISTENCE OF THE TWO APPROACHES

Hence it was possible for the two approaches, Augustinian and Aristotelian-Boethian, to coexist, and this coexistence could be fruitful. Both approaches ran the risk of encouraging separation and fragmentation, for different reasons; but so long as neither approach clearly had the upper hand, the existence of the one put some kind of limit on the dangerous tendencies of the other. We should not forget that Aristotelian logical and metaphysical notions were (and are) used in expressing the doctrine of the Church, to which writers adopting either approach subscribed. Thus those who followed an Augustinian approach had an interest in continuing to strive to adopt and incorporate developments made in the Aristotelian-Boethian approach – after all, this incorporation was part of the Augustinian project. Meanwhile, writers with and Aristotelian-Boethian approach were, after all, believers, and interested, like the Augustinians, in serving the understanding of faith as well as in developing their own understanding of language and the world.

The tension continued unresolved, though, occasionally causing problems such as those in which Abelard found himself. But this very tension encouraged people to want to try to overcome the difficulties and to strive after harmony, reconciliation and synthesis. It was, after all, the claim of the Augustinian approach that all human wisdom could be judged by those who had the understanding based on faith, and either be definitively incorporated into that understanding, or, in the light of it, be definitively rejected. Meanwhile within the Aristotelian-Boethian approach the aim was to see how far the reason could get towards the full truth revealed by God, before that revelation was made. There need therefore have been no contradiction, in principle, between the conclusions reached by either approach; and while the tendencies towards the separation of faith and reason which existed within both traditions could be held in check, solid work could be done to resolve any apparent contradiction.

We should not forget that medieval authors thought of the philosophical task as one which continues through tradition over the generations: each generation might be expected to go some way to resolving the difficulties bequeathed to it by the generation before, but might also be expected to throw up new difficulties, in its turn, for the next generation to try to resolve. Medieval thinkers did not expect to be able to solve all difficulties by one stroke of genius, within the means available to them; that is, within the tradition of the craft at the stage of development and improvement towards its ultimate perfection at which it then happened to be. They did not hope to hand on to the next generation anything better than the best result achieved so far.

As long as the tendencies to separation within each approach were held in check, the tensions set up between the rival approaches could continue to be fruitful. The question was: how long could they be held in check? It is sad to relate that the development of the university seems to have played a part in removing what checks there were. The university is – or perhaps was – in some ways the most excellent of medieval inventions: a powerful institution in which the development of intellectual tradition could be protected and encouraged. But it also fostered destruction.

The University of Bologna goes back to 1158, while the University of Paris, which was the chief centre of philosophy, dates from 1215. They were institutions which ensured the presence in one place of many scholars and masters working within different approaches to the tradition: this should have made possible the interaction which would make sure that separation between the two approaches, and separation between reason and faith within either approach, could never reach a point of danger. The Augustinians would be continually presented by the Aristotelians with new developments which they would need to interpret and judge; and this interpretation and judgement would help set a valuable limit to the speculations of the Aristotelians.

Indeed, we have seen something of the sort happening in the case of Abelard. This occurred before the foundation of the University of Paris, but there already existed in his time a kind of academic community, the 'Paris schools', from which the University grew. Abelard's solution to the logical-metaphysical problem of the universals could be absorbed into the tradition, up to a point: in fact, even his highly conservative and Augustinian contemporary Hugo of St Victor (d. 1141) accepted it. But when Abelard went further than this and tried to use his logical discoveries and speculations as a source of truth that could be used to correct the traditional understanding of the faith, he had gone too far. He was told he had gone too far, and he accepted the rebuke.

But even in this story there are signs of danger. It was not the academic community, principally, that rebuked Abelard: it was St Bernard, coming in from outside, wielding immense spiritual prestige and appealing to Church authority. Abelard had been rebuked and accused of heresy by other masters all his life; but it seems as if he regarded this as no more than the hurly-burly of academic debate. Like the gangster portrayed by Edward G. Robinson in the film *Little Caesar*, he could take it as well as dish it out, and he could dish it out as well as take it. He had a well-founded belief that he was in fact more intelligent than any of the masters who criticised him. Debate between more-or-less equals is not always, or perhaps even not often, the best way to resolve important theoretical disagreements, especially when the debating equals are intelligent, of strong character, and zealous for the development of their own studies.

This brings us to the real weakness of the medieval university, which grew up out of academic communities like that of the Paris schools. The very constitution of the university can lead towards a separation of approaches, and a fragmentation of traditions. This may have been more marked in universities which were renowned for more practical studies, such as Bologna with its reputation for law, and Salerno with its reputation for medicine; particularly as these universities were in origin associations of students. But the same tendency could be found even in universities which were associations of masters, and where theology and philosophy predominated, such as Paris and its offshoot Oxford. The University of Paris was set up on the Augustinian plan of seeking understanding based on faith, and was perhaps more immediately inspired by the *Didascalion* of Hugo of St Victor. But even in Paris the university consisted of more or less autonomous faculties. The faculty of Arts, on the Augustinian model, was seen as providing the necessary tools for the development of the understanding of faith which was taught in the faculty of Theology. But they were still two different faculties; and they soon developed two different groups of masters. All the features of university politics began to grow up as well. We live in a fallen world.

The masters of the faculty of Arts were perhaps in an invidious position: if they explicitly related their teachings to the faith they would be accused of usurping the rights of the faculty of Theology. But if they did not, the danger could arise of their teaching merely pagan wisdom in a pagan way, teaching their subjects without regard to how they could be incorporated into the understanding of faith. Since the teaching of logic and dialectic fell within the task of the faculty of Arts, the masters there would tend to adopt the Aristotelian approach; and since, sad to say, academics are quite often at least as concerned about the prestige and status of their faculties as they are about the truth, there is little doubt that most of the masters of Theology preferred things that way. That is, they preferred that the logicians should stick to logic and not presume to reflect on questions of faith. But this attitude would breed a reaction. If the theologians were unwilling to allow the logicians to trespass on their preserves, the logicians would, by a universal tendency of human nature, try to keep the theologians and their considerations well out of the faculty of Arts.

Perhaps Hugo of St Victor had seen something of a separation of this kind occurring already in the Paris schools which preceded the university, and as a result wrote his *Didascalion* to recall the masters to the need for a unity of project. It may be that the ideas put forward by Hugo in this book had an influence on those who amalgamated the different schools into a single university. But it is clear that the masters of Arts were not always content with the role Hugo assigned to them, or were not always fully conscious of its importance.

There were attempts by various figures to recall them to a due consciousness, and for a time the University throve in some kind of unity, if not always harmony. It is not clear how long this could have lasted. But in any case there was no chance: for at this stage the re-discovered works of Aristotle broke on the scene.

5.5 THE CHALLENGE OF THE DISCOVERY OF ARISTOTLE

In spite of everything, the tradition still continued, served by the rival approaches and by their clashings. The Augustinian approach had the upper hand, at least in Paris, and when that hand was used wisely the Augustinian approach could still continue to adopt, adapt and reconcile the new developments that might appear, either from within itself or from within the Aristotelian approach. But in the late twelfth and early thirteenth centuries the balance of power was shaken, and a whole mass of new teachings suddenly appeared: a mass that it was beyond the power of the current generation of masters either to incorporate into the tradition or to reject. This set up a whole new set of problems that needed to be answered: the gentle, step-by-step attitude implied in the development of a tradition seemed to be insufficient. This mass of new teachings was Aristotle's philosophy taken as a whole.

Here was a whole new system of human wisdom. The Augustinian approach demanded that it should be possible to incorporate this into the understanding based on faith, or to show why it should be rejected. Total rejection was impossible. Aristotle's was already a name with authority within the tradition: all the logic of Augustinian scholars was based on his, one way or another, and they included some of his concepts in the definitions of their faith that were recited in church every Sunday and major feast day. Nor could the task be put off, or taken little by little.

For if the theologians and Augustinians were slow, the logicians and Aristotelians would not be. Here was new material which fitted exactly with what they already knew and taught. If the theologians were unwilling to incorporate this material, why, so much the better: it would lead to the work of incorporation and assimilation being left to the faculty of Arts, where they taught; and they were confident of their powers to carry out this work. It would enable them to get to grips with major philosophical problems without being told that they were poaching on the preserves of the faculty of Theology.

We have seen that the Neoplatonists, and the Augustinians who followed them, had no difficulty in incorporating Aristotle's logic into their systems. In Abelard's time it seemed as if developments of that logic, and the underlying metaphysics along Aristotelian lines, might have posed a danger to the Augustinian understanding: but the danger was averted, and the new developments in logic were incorporated in their turn. But now thinkers in the West were for the first time presented, in a fully developed form, with the metaphysics and the theory of knowledge that underpinned that logic. They fitted the familiar logic, of course; and they fitted it far better than the Neoplatonic and Augustinian metaphysics and theories of knowledge on to which they had been grafted. To accept them into the Augustinian synthesis would have meant a massive reworking either of Aristotle's metaphysics and theory of knowledge, or of Augustine's. It was hard to see how a synthesis could be achieved that would not simply be a conquest of one by the other, or at least a radical re-translation of the one in terms of the other. If Augustinianism could not achieve a synthesis, then its pretensions to provide a universal understanding on the basis of faith were overthrown; but if it merely flattened the claims of Aristotelianism on grounds of authority, or provided a radical translation of Aristotelianism into its own terms, this would leave the Aristotelians of the Arts faculty dissatisfied and alienated, and ready at the first opportunity to rebel and work up Aristotelian theories independently. Authority did at times try to forbid the reading of Aristotle – there is a story that at one time the University of Toulouse attempted to attract students with the bait 'Come to Toulouse and read the works of Aristotle that are forbidden in Paris'. In quite a short time such heavy-handed attempts to stamp out the study of Aristotle failed. What could be done?

The Augustinian position itself demanded that it should be able to give some account of this rival. The aim of the Augustinian project was a synthesis of all human wisdom. Any suggestion put forward for inclusion in that synthesis, in principle, could be judged in the light of that wisdom. If true, it could be incorporated; if false, it could be shown to be false and rejected. It looked, at this time, as if the philosophy of Aristotle could neither be incorporated nor rejected. Medieval thinkers were all too prone to accuse their opponents of teaching that there could be two separate kinds of truth, a religious truth and a truth of reason. Any thinker who did so hold would have been guilty of abandoning the Augustinian project (as well as the Aristotelian logic which structured it), and it is in fact hard to pin down any medieval thinker as actually having made such a radical claim. But we do have, from the period, the notes of an anonymous student who was confused enough by the problems of the age to note 'The above [Aristotelian] propositions are true in the Faculty of Arts, but not in the Faculty of Divinity'. The problem was a real and a serious one.

6

THE DISCOVERY
OF ARISTOTLE

6.1 ARISTOTELIAN CONCEPTS

6.1.1 *Individuals and Universals*

Perhaps the best way in which we can approach the problem which was presented to the medieval intellectual world by the rediscovery of the works of Aristotle is to look at a few of Aristotle's teachings: those that presented most difficulty to their medieval readers, those that are most unfamiliar or easiest to misinterpret for the modern reader, and those which had most influence and currency in the Middle Ages. Nearly all the philosophical notions which are to be found expressed in medieval literature, or which applied in one way or another in the actions and structures dealt with in medieval history, are of Aristotelian origin. We can perhaps best begin from the new light cast by the newly-rediscovered writings on concepts which medieval thinkers had already derived from Aristotle through Boethius.

We have already seen something of Aristotle's terminology on the notions of substance and accident. As was noted earlier, the doctrines which he expresses in his logical works, which Boethius translated, still need a lot of explanation. For a start, Aristotle seems to have left unexplained the relationship between individual substances and the kinds to which they belong. The 'problem of the universals', which was touched on above, had to do with the investigation of this relationship. Despite difficulties it might occasion for their logic, it was still open to thinkers in the Neoplatonic tradition to hold that the relationship between individuals and the kinds they belong to was the sort of relationship Plato had suggested: a relationship of participation in, or of likeness to, transcendent Platonic Ideas or Forms. Augustinians, as we have seen, while tending to accept a fundamentally Platonic answer to the problem, substituted for Plato's Forms – which existed in their own right – ideas or exemplars in the creative mind of God.

The 'debate on the universals' was a discussion of the logical corollaries of this metaphysical doctrine. It took the form of asking 'How do the words we use relate either to individuals or to kinds?' An intermediate answer, between Platonism and nominalism, was developed, and became widely accepted. Both extreme Platonism (also known as 'extreme realism') and extreme nominalism came to be generally rejected. The former held that our language relates directly and solely to the Forms or divine exemplars, so that the word 'white', for example, did not stand for or strictly apply to anything white in the world, but only to the divine idea of whiteness, by likeness to which God made all things that we see as white to be more or less, but not strictly, white. The latter held that our language relates solely to individuals: thus, the word 'white' is just another name that we apply to e.g. this cloud, this daisy-petal, this patch of snow, besides the names of 'cloud', 'daisy-petal', 'patch of snow'. But now the metaphysical doctrines behind Aristotle's logical teachings became known, and threw the debate open again.

6.1.2 Form and Matter

The exact correct interpretation of Aristotle on this subject was hotly debated in medieval times, and is still debated today. But at least it seems certain that Aristotle in fact held that in every substance there is *something in virtue of which* it belongs to the kind it belongs to. Kinds are therefore not mere human constructions, which counts against the nominalist view. But this 'something in the individual in virtue of which it belongs to its kind' is also developed by Aristotle in a strongly anti-Platonic way. It is true that he uses for this notion a word Plato sometimes used, 'form'. This is from an ordinary Greek word meaning 'shape', but it is not the same word as the one Plato usually uses which was translated above as 'Form' (with a capital) or 'Idea'. But the Aristotelian notion of form itself is clearly meant to be something quite opposed to Plato's conceptions. Plato's 'Form' is something entirely distinct from any individual entity in this world: it is only by more-or-less resembling this transcendent Form that individuals can have the name of the Form applied to them. Snow is white because it resembles the White.

For Aristotle this is quite wrong. Snow is really white, because the form white is part of the snow. A human being is really a human being, not because it resembles, more or less, some super-Human Being somewhere outside the world, but because what it is to be a human being, the form of human being, is what this human being is.

Aristotle develops his doctrine in answer to Plato, but also as part of an on-going debate which dates back to before Plato and even Socrates. The early Greek philosophers were always asking what the most basic existents were. One answer, which in general style if not in detail is still popular today, was that all the things we see around us are combinations of much simpler and basic entities – 'atoms', the Greeks used to call them. Now we might say 'quarks' or 'superstrings'. Another sort of answer was that all the things we see around us are different manifestations of some very basic stuff. The ancient Greeks suggested water or fire: nowadays one might say 'energy'. The scientific and philosophical endeavours were not then as distinct as they have become, and even today are not so distinct as some people would like to think they are.

Aristotle was impatient with this kind of answer, no less than with Platonic doctrines. The notion which he twins with 'form' is 'matter'. Just as he wants to insist, against Plato, that a human being is what a human being really is, and not something supra-natural that ordinary humans resemble, so he wants to say against they earlier natural philosophers that a human being really is a human being and not just a collection of atoms. The human being does not consist of the same stuff all the time, it is true: Aristotle says that the form of this human being takes on different matter at different times – by, for example, eating. Also the human being may die: in this case the form will disappear, leaving the matter to take on other forms. A thing is what it is in virtue of a form, and there is at no time matter which has no form. But there is no form that the matter has to have.

This pair of concepts is not as confusing as may at first appear. The notions involved are ones which we all use quite naturally as part of our common-sense metaphysics. They may be difficult to understand because one is looking for something abstract and complex: in fact, Aristotle's doctrine, when properly understood, should be a rather boring disappointment. The correct reaction on having properly grasped most of Aristotle's metaphysics is not 'Aha!' but 'Oh, is that all?' Good philosophy, and certainly good metaphysics, is often a matter of clearly expressing something already known.

Aristotle distinguishes, we might say, between the stuff that makes up a substance at any time, which he calls its matter, and the way in which that stuff is organised or structured to make that substance. This 'way in which the stuff is organised' he calls the form. The simplest way to understand the distinction is to notice an analogy which he himself uses between natural things and artificial things. If we think of an artificial unit, such as a bundle of sticks, we can distinguish matter and form quite easily. The matter is what the bundle is made up of, a number of sticks and a piece of string; while the form is what makes these sticks and this string to be a bundle: i.e. the tying. The same sticks and string could exist without being a bundle, by existing just as a pile of sticks with a piece of string on top, or by being made into a rudimentary birdcage. This would be the same matter with a different form. But any individual stick in the bundle could be removed and substituted by another, without untying; indeed, you could replace all the sticks that way, taking one out and putting a new one in, without untying and thus destroying the bundle, and you would be left in some sense with the same bundle. This would be the same form with different matter.

This distinction can be carried across to natural things. If we think again of the cat Ludo, which we used as an example of an individual substance in the last chapter, we want to distinguish between the stuff or matter that happens to make up Ludo at a given moment. The stuff which makes up Ludo could very well have gone to make up something else, just as the sticks and string of the bundle could have been put together to form a crude bird-cage. Suppose I have two cats, Ludo and Ludwig, born in the same litter and brought up by me since they left their mother. I have fed them separately, Ludo on Brand X of cat-food, Ludwig on Brand Y. If I had decided instead to feed Ludo on Brand Y and Ludwig on Brand X then the stuff that in fact now goes to make up Ludo would have gone to make up Ludwig, and vice-versa. The fact that I have given the example in terms of different kinds of cat-food is of course irrelevant: a little thought will show that even if I had fed them out of the same tin, the same point could have been made, provided that no amount of food eaten by the one was eaten as well by the other. As their metabolisms continue to work, the stuff which makes them up at this moment will be expelled and replaced by new stuff which I kindly provide for them. Moreover, when Ludo dies the stuff he is then made up of will remain. Ludo will have ceased to exist, but the matter will not have ceased to exist. It will, however, have ceased to be a cat.

To continue the analogy, we can try to illustrate the distinction between form and matter in the following way. To ask 'What makes a bundle a bundle?' admits of two answers. In one sense the bundle just is the sticks and the string: there is nothing else, in this sense, that a bundle is besides sticks and string. It is not, for example, sticks and string and a first-class stamp and an address label: that is not a bundle but a badly-made and not very interesting parcel. In another sense, what makes these sticks and this string into a bundle is just the tying: we could say it is the tying that makes the bundle the bundle. In the same way, Ludo in one sense is just this flesh and these bones; in another sense, what Ludo is is what makes this flesh-and-bone stuff to be structured into a cat.

It is important to notice, though, a point at which the analogy between artificial things and natural substances breaks down. Sticks, in or out of a bundle, are still sticks. They have a definite nature or kind in their own right, quite independently of their being brought together or not in the artificial unity we call a bundle. But Aristotle holds that the matter which makes up Ludo is not in the same way in itself of any definite kind or nature, independent of its making up the natural unity of the cat at a particular time, or making up some other natural unity, such as half a canful of cat-food, at another. At the moment, the stuff that makes up Ludo is stuff of a definite kind: cat-stuff, the stuff of a cat. Indeed, we can perfectly well say that what this stuff is is a cat, and also what Ludo is, in one sense. But if Ludo suddenly dies the same stuff will stop being a cat or cat-stuff, and become a cat corpse or cat-corpse stuff. And a cat corpse is something of quite a different nature from a cat, it is something of an entirely different kind. (Indeed, some Aristotelians would have held that a corpse is not one thing at all, but only a loose collection of different things, the collection becoming looser and looser as the thing decays. But be that as it may, a cat corpse or dead cat is not at all the same kind of thing as a cat is. When people see the dead body of someone they know, a frequent reaction is to recognise this fact, and even to say 'That's not him'.)

At any time, then, the matter is something or other definite; but there is nothing definite that it is *all* the time. Here Aristotle expresses his disagreement with the pre-Socratic philosophers. They thought that there must be some basic definite kind of stuff – atoms, earth, air, fire or water, or some combination of these – which everything really was all the time. For Aristotle, when the matter is cat-food it is cat-food and nothing else; when it is a cat it is a cat and nothing else; and when it is a cat-corpse, whatever that is, it is a cat corpse and nothing else.

This leaves us with a difficulty in answering the question 'what is matter?' since giving any definite answer will precisely undermine the distinctively Aristotelian notion. But we can say that matter is that in a substance which is capable of becoming a different substance, or other substances. We might even say that this matter just is this substance in so far as this substance can become another substance or other substances. In the same way the sticks and the string are that in the bundle which is capable of becoming a different bundle, or parts of different bundles, or a birdcage. Or again, we can say that in a sense these sticks and this string just are this bundle in so far as it can become a different bundle, or parts of different bundles. Form, by contrast, is that in a substance in virtue of which it is a substance of the kind that it is. Or we could even say that the form just is this substance in so far as it is a substance of that kind. The analogy between the natural and the artificial continues to apply: the tying of the bundle is that in virtue of which the bundle is a bundle, and not a heap or a birdcage. The tying, in this sense, just is the bundle in so far as it is a bundle and not e.g. a birdcage.

This discussion brings us back round again to the problem of what are the relationships between an individual substance and the kind that it belongs to. If we consider the two cats, Ludo and Ludwig, it is clear that they are two different lumps of stuff, different amounts of matter; that they are, in technical language, materially different. But it is also obvious that these two amounts of matter are organised in some sense in the same way. It is, in some sense, therefore, the same form that makes these two lumps of stuff to be two different individual substances of the same kind. They are both cats, that is.

However, it should be equally clear that in a different sense, since Ludo and Ludwig are two different substances, two different cats, they each have their own individual structure: though they are both cats, they are two different cats and two different cats are two different amounts of matter each separately organised. Consider the analogy of the artificial unity of the bundle again. If I have two bundles, it is in virtue of the same thing, tying, that they are both bundles. But since they are two different bundles, made up of two different collections of sticks that exist separately at one and the same time, and also two different bits of string, it should also be clear that there are two different tyings involved.

It is annoying, but perhaps natural, that Aristotle and the medieval Aristotelians should have used one and the same word, 'form', in both these two senses: the sense in which there is one form in the two cats because they are both cats, and the sense in which there are two different forms because they are two different cats. In the one sense, Ludo and Ludwig have the same form. They must have: the matter that makes them up has to be organised or structured in the same way (in some sense of 'the same way'), or else they could not both be cats. But in another sense they must have two different forms, for if not they would be one and the same cat. The reader of medieval philosophers and of those influenced by them should always be on guard against possible confusions which the authors may cause or may themselves be suffering from in this way.

This distinction of form and matter is of enormous importance, both philosophically and in medieval culture at large. A medieval thinker tended to analyse any phenomenon in terms of its form and its matter, often applying the notions in what may seem to us far-fetched connections. It can be used, as we have used it, both of natural things and of artificial things. It is used even in logic: Aristotelians would speak of the subject of a sentence, what the sentence is about, as the 'matter' of the sentence, while comparing the predicate – that which is said about the subject – to the form. Or again, in a logical argument, the individual sentences which form the premisses and the conclusion are the matter, while the way they are linked together to give a valid or invalid conclusion is the form. This piece of Aristotelian jargon is still used by contemporary logicians, despite all the advances made in logic since Aristotle's time, when they speak of valid or invalid 'forms' of argument.

6.1.3 Analogy

I mentioned that some of the usages of this notion might seem to us far-fetched. Perhaps the examples given above seem far-fetched. Some simply seem to us incorrect, as when Aristotle insists that units are the matter of numbers. But medieval authors had given a lot of thought to the question of the stretching and transferring of concepts and terminology, and developed extremely subtle accounts of how sense can be transferred without being lost.

Contemporary logicians tend to aim at the clear-cut nature of mathematical language: there are historical and philosophical reasons or excuses for this, but they need not concern us here. As a result, any expression which cannot be given a definite and unambiguous meaning tends to be rejected as ambiguous or vague or fuzzy. Most of the expressions we use to describe the world in ordinary and even in scientific discourse tends to be a little fuzzy, a little ill-defined around the edges, and so some logicians are now turning their attention to fuzziness. But the drive still seems to be to establish at least non-fuzzy limits to the fuzzy areas. Aristotle, by the way, says explicitly at one point that to look for the certainty and definiteness of mathematics in dealing with e.g. human behaviour is the sign of a defective education, and as stupid as it would be to accept the sort of vague and plausible arguments we hear in politics or in the law-courts when doing mathematics.

Medieval philosophers, impelled partly by theological considerations, thought that a dichotomy between the unambiguous and the ambiguous (and therefore useless) was too crude. They spoke of 'univocal' expressions, which correspond to our notion of the unambiguous, and of 'equivocal' expressions, which correspond to the ambiguous: but they did think that in some cases equivocalness or equivocity could be identified, and such expressions used in philosophical, theological scientific discourse, provided due care were exercised. But they also had the notion of 'analogous' expressions: expressions which could be used in a whole range of systematically connected senses, expressions which were thus neither purely univocal nor purely equivocal. Aristotle seems to have regarded most important philosophical terminology as subject to analogous uses, and medieval thinkers followed him. This, as has been mentioned, was partly for theological reasons. It would be foolish to think that when we say God is good we mean exactly the same by 'good' as when we say 'Socrates is good': but we do mean more than if we merely said 'God is not bad' or 'God is the cause of all goodness in the world' or even 'God is X', where all we can say about being X is that it is something God is.

Beyond analogy came metaphor, and here again, again for theological reasons, medieval authors had a subtle account. Metaphor is literally false. The Bible says that God is a rock, but God is not a rock. But there is some element in the meaning of the literally false predicate ' – is a rock' which can truly be applied to God, and the trick of the good Bible scholar or preacher is to bring this out. A rock is firm and relatively unchangeable: God is absolutely unchangeable. A rock is reliable – it is always there and you can lean against it without it giving way – and so is God.

6.1.4 *Explanation and Causality*

Between analogy and metaphor, then, almost any important philosophical expression can have applications far outside its original field. This is perhaps particularly true of the notions of matter and form. One important application or extension of this pair of notions, however, is a quite close one, a strictly philosophical one, and itself one of wide cultural importance. This is its application in the Aristotelian account of explanation or causality.

When contemporary philosophers use the words 'cause' or 'causality', they tend to think of the kind of causality of which the movement of one billiard ball being knocked by another is a good example; in general, they tend to think of one thing knocking into or pushing another. In fact they often go further and speak of causality as being a relationship between two events, rather than between two things. They think of causality as a relationship between the collision of the billiard balls and the beginning to move of the second billiard ball, rather than as a relationship between the two billiard balls. This is quite different from Aristotle's account of causality, which is why many contemporary commentators on Aristotle prefer to talk about Aristotle's theory of explanation.

Be that as it may – and there are points to be made for or against either terminology and either kind of theory – Aristotle holds that there are at least four principal ways in which we can explain, for example, why a given thing exists. We can explain it, first of all, by saying what it is made of. This is explanation on the side of matter, or what medieval writers called 'material cause' or some such phrase. What makes a bundle of sticks a bundle of sticks? we may ask. One kind of answer will be mention the sticks and the string. But another kind will mention the structure, the way in which the stuff or matter that the bundle is made of is organised to make up a bundle of sticks. In this case the explanation will be the tying. This is called explanation on the side of form, or 'formal cause'. These two are, for Aristotle, perhaps the most important elements in any explanation, and they are both ignored or tacitly presupposed by the contemporary theory of causality. We have explained the two notions above: here it is enough to notice that Aristotle thinks that matter and form, or something analogous to them, can and should enter into the explanation of any existent, whether it be a substantial or accidental, natural or artificial, or coincidental phenomenon.

But the explanation of the bundle is not complete merely by giving these two. We can ask how the bundle came to be a bundle, which is the notion that most closely corresponds to the modern notion of 'cause'. We might call it 'causal explanation' or 'mechanical explanation' or 'explanation on the side of the agent'. Aristotle and his heirs call it 'efficient causality', or some such phrase. In the example given, the answer might be the woodcutter who tied up the sticks with the string to make the bundle. Lastly there is a question of what a bundle is for, what it exists for in the first place. The answer here is explanation on the side of the point of the thing, of what the thing is for. Aristotle and his heirs call it 'final cause', or some such phrase.

6.1.5 Finality

Aristotle holds that we can seek for all these kinds of explanation whenever seeking an explanation is appropriate. The one which is likely to present least difficulty to the average contemporary reader is that of efficient causality, and material and formal causality have already been dealt with. That leaves us with final causality, explanation of a thing in terms of its point, and this notion is likely to prove difficult to swallow to the contemporary reader. We are probably willing to admit that we can seek for a point or purpose for artificial things like bundles, but find odd the idea that we can do so for natural things. What can be said in defence of the idea? It looks ridiculously archaic – as if everything had a little soul inside it which has some purpose in mind – or unnecessarily theistic, as if God has a purpose for each thing. The medieval philosophers did indeed believe that God has a purpose for each thing, but they distinguished this notion from that of final causality, and this fact is liable to leave contemporary readers wondering what sense can be attached to their notion of final causality at all.

We can begin to understand the notion by observing that there are a great many natural things that not only can be described or explained in terms of their point; they have to be so described or explained if the description is to be in any degree nearly complete. Parts of organic wholes, for example, such as the parts of the human or other animal bodies, or of other living things, cannot be described properly at all without mention of their function – that is, their point – within the life of the whole organism to which they belong. The notion of there being a point for things in the natural world, then, is not after all a piece of archaic superstition masquerading as science, nor yet a cheap trick to get people to believe in God. It was used in the latter way in the eighteenth century, and in this use was successfully demolished in the nineteenth. This latter modern misuse has nothing to do with the legitimate Aristotelian notion of final causality. The point or function of the human liver, say, is as much a scientific fact as its shape or weight.

The reader might grant this, but will perhaps find it difficult to admit that substances as wholes can have their own point. Aristotle seems to be illegitimately extending considerations which are appropriate in the case of parts of organisms to the universe as a whole. A cat's liver has a point in the cat's life as a whole. To ask what the point of the cat is seems to suppose that the universe as a whole is a sort of organism of which the cat is a part, and there seems no reason for supposing this. Without such a supposition the whole notion seems to fall down. What is the point of a cat? seems to us a fairly senseless question, like 'what is the point of a tiger?' or 'what is the point of an oak tree?'

Popular or pious writers, in the Middle Ages as today, are apt to ignore the conceptual problems involved here, or to cut the knot by appealing to God's purpose or design. We cannot see what the point of a tiger is, but we can be sure that God made it for a purpose, that it is part of God's design, and it therefore has a point. When they are basing themselves more on the Bible than on Aristotle they are apt to say that the point of all these things is to serve the human race. This works well enough for cats and for oak-trees, though such remarks are not very politically correct, but is a little far-fetched when applied to tigers. Grosseteste, for example, followed Augustine in arguing that tigers are there to punish us for our sins and to instil the fear of God into us by making us recognise how powerful even one of God's creatures is.

This, I would say, is fine in a sermon if convincingly put across – the difficulty being precisely that of putting it across convincingly. But this popular or pious notion of God's purpose or design is not Aristotle's notion of the point of things, of final causality. (It is arguably not good theology, either: God's purposes or designs are inscrutable to us even when God has revealed something of them. The Book of Job is canonical evidence for this. The wild beasts and monsters are mentioned there to show how we cannot second-guess God's designs, not as examples of how clear God's designs are. Job has no idea why God made Leviathan, but he is expected to admit, as he does, that there must be some good reason beyond his comprehension.)

Conscious design or purpose applied to a thing may not coincide with the natural point of that thing. I may use an acorn to throw at someone at a picnic, but this conscious purpose or design of mine, of teasing the target, is not what an acorn is for, not what its point is. The point of an acorn is to grow up into an oak tree: that is what it is for. An acorn, and in general any part of the apparatus for the reproduction of plants and animals, is one of those things that cannot be adequately described, let alone explained, without mention of what it is for. On the other hand, my design or purpose in throwing the acorn at someone I like or dislike, is not in the least relevant to our being able to describe the acorn as an acorn, with a view to explaining what it is.

A point worth bringing out at this stage is that at least in these cases we require some mention of what a thing is for even if we are to state what it is, let alone to explain it. There are cases, then, where final causality enters necessarily into a statement of what a thing is. Final causality, that is, may be closely related to formal causality: both may be necessary to state what a thing is, as part of explaining it. This notion is one that Aristotelians use a great deal, and tend to be laughed at nowadays for doing so. But leaving aside acorns, there are a couple of concepts we use every day which are defined almost wholly in terms of what they are for: woman and man, female and male. Being female or male is not a matter of three-dimensional geometry – what sticks out and what is hollow, as it were. It happens to be so in our species, but we can imagine discovering a thoroughly alien species on Mars. To discover if they are sexed, and if so, how, we need to know more than the geometry: we need to know the function of the different individuals in continuing the life of the species.

Staying with reproduction, we can find a way of extending the notion of things' having a point more widely in the natural world than the organic parts of plants and animals which we began with. Acorns cannot be fully described or explained without mention of what they are for, for propagating the next generation of oak trees. Can we fully describe a mature oak tree without mentioning acorns? I think not: a sterile oak tree is an imperfect specimen, and to describe a perfect specimen we have to mention its breeding capacities. We certainly cannot fully describe a mature oak tree without some mention of its part in the life of the species as a whole. If we were describing both oaks and hollies we would have to say that oaks, like most trees, are hermaphrodite, while hollies are sexually differentiated. Indeed, if we think of an oak tree in the forest rather than in a suburban back garden we should probably have to make some mention, in giving a complete description of the oak tree, of the part it plays in the life of the forest as a whole: the ecosystem, as people say nowadays. Thus we can hold that even a mature oak tree has a point: a point which we can read off, to a certain extent, from what oak trees characteristically do.

The point to notice here is that 'what a thing characteristically does' is something that can be said of almost anything. If final causality can be read off from characteristic activity, then we have a reason to apply the notion of final causality to any natural whole: not merely to parts of plants and animals, nor merely to individual plants or animals relative to the life of the species.

It is true that a part of the characteristic activities of oak trees, perhaps the most characteristic activity is that they grow acorns. We seem to be going in a circle, if acorns are for oak trees and oak trees are for acorns. But the circle is not a vicious one. The circle is equivalent to the life of the species, and that is what both individual oak trees and individual acorns are for. We may then be emboldened to ask what the point of the life of the species as a whole is, and the question is a good one. But no answer need be given or sought at this time: it is enough that we have shown that natural wholes, as well as parts of natural things and artificial wholes, can be said to have a point.

Notice again how closely the explanation in terms of a thing's point is related to the explanation in terms of form. It is in virtue of its form – its structure – that a substance is the kind of substance that it is. It is therefore in virtue of its form that it is able to carry out the characteristic activities of things of that kind. Meanwhile, explanation in terms of what the thing is for can be reached from a consideration of these characteristic activities. Being a substance, then, involves having a form, which involves having a characteristic set of activities, and thus having a point. Part of that point, in the case of living things, will be propagating according to that form, propagating things of that kind and that structure. All these ideas, then, are linked.

We get the most interesting cases where there are clearly other characteristic activities, besides that of propagating, as in the case of human beings. Human beings alone, so far as we know, are capable of rational thought, and of directing their actions according to rational considerations. These characteristic activities are thus appropriately considered as part of what human beings are for, according to Aristotelians.

We need to go behind the notion of activity, characteristic or not, to that of the capacity for an activity. Most acorns never grow into oak trees, though growing into an oak tree is what an acorn is for. An acorn is none the less an acorn just because it happens never to grow into an oak tree, because I have brought it home as a souvenir of my picnic and put it on my mantlepiece. Growing into an oak tree is still what it is for, even if it never achieves its point: if not, as we saw, it could not be properly described as an acorn. We have to conclude that the actual achievement of the point is not necessary for a thing to have that point. What it does need, though, is to have the capacity for achieving that point. A human being is no less a human being, and is for what human beings are for, just because the exercise of its capacity, the achievement of its point, is in some way obstructed by illness or early death or handicap. If the capacity is there, the life is a human life, though not perhaps a very fortunate or successful one.

Capacities are always defined in terms of the activity that they are capacities for: always defined in terms of their exercise. If whenever we identify an activity (and especially a characteristic activity) we can postulate a capacity, then we have managed to put back final causality, what things are for, at the heart of our description of the world. Everything acts: non-living agents are none the less agents. If we identify their activities, we are also attributing to them a capacity. That capacity needs defining in terms of what it is a capacity for: i.e., capacities are defined in terms of what they are for, of their point. It is simply not true that modern science has no use for the notion of finality or capacity: rather, it takes these notions for granted. Modern physics is very different from Aristotle's physics: but it has always been an Aristotelian project, a use of Aristotle's methodology to correct Aristotle's mistakes.

6.1.6 Form and Thought

Returning to the case of human beings, the most characteristic activities of the human being, in Aristotelian philosophy, are thought and the rational direction of action. Thus an essential part of being human is to have at least the capacity, however impaired, to acquire the capacities to perform these characteristic activities. When we turn to consider the activity of thought we find that the notion of form comes in again, in a different way.

It is in virtue of what we are, and therefore of our own form, that we think. It is also, according to Aristotle, in virtue of the forms of the things that we think of that we are able to think of them. This formulation is perhaps not very clear. Aristotle was struck by the fact that the word 'cat', say, can be said of any cat indiscriminately. The use of the word 'cat' on its own makes no reference to any difference between this cat and that cat. This is where the connection arises between a thought and the form of the thing thought of. As we have seen, the difference between this cat and that cat arises from a difference of matter. the two cats are two different lumps of stuff that have one and the same form, in one sense of the word 'form'. Aristotle therefore claims that the thought or concept which we express by the word 'cat' must be in some important way related to the one form that different cats have, rather than to their different matter.

Our thought, then, for Aristotle is non-material and formal. We can see that this must be the case, he and his heirs think, when we consider that it is possible for us to think of anything that exists or can exist. If our mind were in any way material then its capacity for thought – for receiving the forms of the things we think of – would be in some way restricted by the characteristics of the matter that made it up. The eye can see all colours, reasons Aristotle, only because it is itself of no colour but transparent. If our eyes were coloured red we would be unable to distinguish what is red from what is white or grey. In the same way, if our minds were material they would be unable to receive certain forms – be unable to think of certain things. The matter of which a cat is made is limited in its receptivity: it cannot become an elephant just like that. It cannot even become part of an elephant, given that elephants are not carnivores, until the corpse of the cat has been broken down and been used to nourish a plant which the elephant might then eat. But our minds can receive the forms of a cat and an elephant – can think of a cat and of an elephant – one after another or simultaneously, with no difficulty. Therefore there can be no material restriction on the receptivity of human minds.

This, according to Aristotelians, is how the mind matches up to the world. It is not by containing or producing a likeness or image that corresponds to the world, but by having in itself, in a non-material mode of existence, the very same forms that exist, albeit in a material mode of existence, in the things we are thinking of. This theory dodges the well-known dangers of an infinite regress starting, when we consider whether our idea of the world corresponds to the world or not. All we end up doing in that theory is comparing our idea of the world with our idea of our idea of the world. Since for the Aristotelian theory there is no likeness or correspondence, but formal identity, the vicious regress never gets started.

6.2 PROBLEMS AND DANGEROUS SOLUTIONS

Even with this over-sketchy account of some of the chief features of the philosophy of Aristotle and his heirs, it will be possible to see why this philosophy was seen as presenting a threat to the Augustinian understanding and tradition. To take the last point dealt with, the Aristotelian theory of thought and knowledge just outlined is entirely at odds with the Augustinian-Platonic system. There appears to be no role in our knowledge, according to Aristotle's philosophy, for the divine exemplars, and thus there is no need for a direct divine illumination for us to reach the truth. Aristotle's account appeared to Augustinians naturalistic, one which excluded God's action from the world. For the Aristotelians, the mind matches the world by its own nature; so the fact of our knowledge of the world does not, as it did for Augustine and his followers, immediately point beyond itself to God.

It was hard for Augustinians to assimilate a teaching such as this. Following Aristotle would lead one to make a very strong distinction between natural modes of knowing and the knowledge that comes by divine enlightenment, by faith. But it was precisely part of the attractiveness of Augustine's idea that understanding follows on faith, that there was, in this picture, no strong distinction but rather a strong analogy between the two kinds of knowledge. If, as Aristotle and his followers seemed to be saying, reason of its own nature was adequate to achieve a complete understanding of at least this world, what became of the Augustinian claim that understanding followed on faith?

The same kind of problem turned up again and again. Aristotle and his followers claimed that by their theories of explanation they could find order and intelligibility in the world as it stood. This was the order and intelligibility that Augustine had found only after receiving the faith, through submission of the intellect and will to God's authority, expressed in and through the Church and the Scriptures. For the Aristotelians, the world was complete and completely ordered, and had a point of its own. Thus it did not seem to point beyond itself so obviously as it did for the Augustinians. Augustine and his followers were forever finding traces, footsteps, even clues or fingerprints, of divinity in the world: in knowledge, in order, in beauty, in finality. Aristotle offered an explanation of all of these as parts of the way the world itself is ordered: he did not need to bring God in at every stage to explain them.

Aristotelian doctrines on the characteristic purpose and the point of human life were also upsetting. Augustine had claimed that God has made us for himself, and our hearts are restless until they rest in him. Aristotle puts forward a theory by which human beings can achieve their point, can fulfil their own nature, and thus achieve perfect happiness, in this life, without any direct intervention from any god. The unity between faith and reason which Augustine and his followers upheld thus seemed to be destroyed: the happiness of heaven appeared to be something extra, tacked on, not part of the real fulfilment of the human being.

This sketch of the difficulties faced by Augustinians when they considered Aristotle may seem exaggerated: but in fact to the Augustinians of the twelfth and early thirteenth century things seemed even worse than this. The sketch just given of the central notions of Aristotelian philosophy is as favourable, from an Augustinian point of view, as can be. In so far as possible, it was couched in terms that Aquinas, who was to attempt the task of synthesizing Aristotle and Augustine, would have used. But Aristotle did not make his first appearance in the West in that guise: the interpretation of Aristotle given above – an interpretation which made the synthesis possible – was not given to Aquinas, but had to be achieved.

For example, Aristotle's explanation of the nature of thought, though it has its attraction, ends up making the whole operation look extraordinary. How is it that there can be non-material capacities and activities in a material being, in an animal such as the human being is? Aristotle was forced to conclude that at least the active part of the intellect – the part that forms concepts, i.e. non-material forms – was something divine. This was perhaps not a problem for a Greek who was used to a plurality of divinities. But for those who believe in one God only, does this doctrine of Aristotle's not mean that God must be thinking in all of us? This would mean that we all share the same mind, God's mind. And if we all share the same mind, how can our individual minds or souls survive our death as individuals, as the Christian faith teaches?

Again, Aristotle's rational explanation of the way the world is structured meant that it might just as well have gone on for ever. In fact Aristotle did believe that it had gone on for ever, that it had not and could not have had a beginning. Where did this leave the first verse of the Bible, 'In the beginning God created the heaven and the earth'?

Aristotle on his own, before he could be given an appropriate Christian interpretation, appeared dangerous enough to Augustinians. What made things worse is that when the texts of Aristotle came into the West they had already received what was from a Christian point of view a highly inappropriate interpretation. These first texts of the rediscovered Aristotle had a quite different appearance from the sketch outlined in the first part of the chapter. They were translations from the Arabic, and were accompanied by Arabic commentaries, since the impact of the rediscovered Aristotle had been felt in the Muslim world before it reached the West.

The Muslim thinkers had been faced with the same kind of difficulty. They had developed from early times their own theological schools of reflection on the teachings of Islam, perhaps originally as a result of contacts with Greek and Christian philosophical schools in Syria. Muslim thinkers, too, had found the impact of Aristotle's complete rational explanation of the world, with no essential part played by God's direct action, a stumbling-block. The great philosopher Ibn Sina (980–1036, known in the West as Avicenna) had attempted to make a synthesis: but in the hurly-burly of school debates his teachings were mostly supplanted by those of the more radical Ibn Rushd (1126–1198; the name is latinised as Averroes.) At the same time Maimonides (Moishe ben Maimon; 1135–1204) was attempting to synthesise Islamic and Aristotelian philosophy with his own Jewish faith.

We may pause for a minute to reflect on the remarkable unity of the intellectual world at this time. Jews were persecuted in various

114

parts of the Christian and Muslim worlds – in Maimonides' lifetime, for example, in England, in Christian Spain, in Muslim Spain, and in the Yemen. Christians and Muslims were fighting each other in Spain, in the Holy Land, and in Asia Minor. There were continual wars between Christian princes in the north and west, and between Muslim princes in the south and east. But despite all this, Avicenna, in Bokhara and Baghdad, Maimonides in Cairo, and Averroes in Cordoba, all contributed to the same debate; and within a generation or so after Maimonides's death, their works, together with the works of Aristotle, were available in Latin translations in Paris and Oxford. Not to mention that one of the principal translators of Averroes, Michael Scot, came from as remote a country as Scotland, and studied Arabic with Jewish teachers in Christian Spain.

But though there was a great deal of unity in the intellectual world, there were important differences. All were seeking to make the learning of Aristotle consistent with religious tradition; but, of course, what is consistent with Muslim or Jewish tradition may not be consistent with Christian tradition. Aristotle as interpreted by Muslims might be doubly dangerous to the Augustinian tradition.

For example, neither Islam nor Judaism seem to have as clear and definite teachings on the life of the world to come as the Christian tradition held or had developed. Solutions to problems such as what is human nature, and how the life of the world to come fulfils it, might thus easily be acceptable in the East, but not in the West. Again, the rather fatalistic answers that seem to have been acceptable to Muslims on questions to do with the relation between God's foreknowledge and human freedom would probably not have been acceptable to Christians or Jews. Indeed, Maimonides, writing for Jews living among Muslims, spends a good deal of effort in attacking fatalism.

In fact Maimonides seems in some ways to have had more success in his task of reconciling the teachings of Aristotle with his religious tradition than the great Muslim thinkers had in their comparable task. His *Guide of the Perplexed* contains many important reflections on God's providence and the world, and how we are able to speak of the infinite and inscrutable God. These doctrines were sometimes taken up and sometimes developed independently, in a parallel way, by the intellectuals of Western Europe who read chiefly in Latin and scarcely at all in Greek. Here, Maimonides was also regarded above all as an authority on the relations between the Law which God gave expressly to his people, and general human ideas of goodness.

Aristotle as interpreted by Averroes, however, seemed to Augustinians not just doubly dangerous – as a heathen interpreted by a Muslim – but even trebly dangerous, as a heathen interpreted by a Muslim who was unorthodox even by the standards of Islam. It seems that Averroes was not altogether successful in achieving a synthesis of faith and reason. He responded to attacks on the Aristotelianism of authors such as Avicenna with a yet more radical Aristotelianism, which seemed even less compatible with the traditional faith of Islam.

Averroes was frequently charged with heresy, or, what is scarcely better, with teaching that there are different and incompatible truths, a truth of reason and a truth of faith, a truth of science and a truth of religion. Particularly upsetting to the faithful was the fact that he apparently believed that the truth of reason was in some way superior. He seems also to have believed that the world had existed from all eternity, as Aristotle had taught. Further, his reading of Aristotle led him to believe that the active, concept-forming part of the mind was not proper to the individual human being, but was one and the same, common to all. This might have seemed acceptable to some, as leaving open a place for direct divine action in human knowing: but it seemed to many, particularly in the West, to close the door to the possibility of the survival of the mind or soul after death, and to the eventual resurrection of the dead.

It seems that the solution of the orthodox defenders of tradition in the East, within Islam and Judaism, was, to a great extent, turn their backs on both Aristotle and philosophy. No great Aristotelian name stands out in the East after these. The position of Avicenna, which was the most likely to be able to achieve a reconciliation between Aristotelianism and Islam, was generally rejected; and the more radical views of Averroes were even less welcome. Unlike Avicenna, who had been the adviser of princes, Averroes had to go into exile to escape persecution from his co-religionists.

Maimonides, meanwhile, though inspiring great devotion among many who knew him (and to this day), aroused fierce opposition among others, an opposition which can also be found today. His contemporary enemies even went to the length of defacing his tomb with the legend 'heretic': I am glad to say it was soon restored. It was left for scholars in the West to try to succeed where those of the East had failed; and they had the failures as well as the successes of Eastern scholars as part of the problem they had to face.

7

REACTIONS
TO ARISTOTLE

7.1 THE EARLY THIRTEENTH CENTURY
AMONG THE THEOLOGIANS

When the statutes of the University of Paris were approved by Papal
authority in 1215 the study of Aristotle's works on natural philosophy and metaphysics was forbidden. The study of his ethics was not
prohibited, while the study of his logic was in fact commanded. This
curiously partial imposition of authority was not a success, as might
have been expected: Aristotle's thought forms a unity, and it makes
little sense to study e.g. the ethics independently of the metaphysics
(as they have been doing at Oxford for centuries and still did in my
day). We find, from a curious compendium of typical examination
questions which has been somehow preserved, that certainly before
1240 all Aristotle's works then available were being studied in the
faculty of Arts. In fact in 1231 the Pope had appointed a commission
of Parisian theologians to investigate the prohibited works: in the
Pope's view, clearly, the intellectual threat needed to be met in an
intellectual way, and not merely by the exercise of legal authority.

Among the members of the commission was, naturally enough,
the archbishop of Paris, William of Auvergne (d. 1249). William's
position was that Aristotle is frequently in error, and then must be
rejected; but that when his doctrines are in conformity with the

118

truths of the Christian faith, they should be accepted. This is to
re-state the ideal of the Augustinian approach to human wisdom.
The question was, though, what in Aristotle was inconsistent and
what consistent with the truths of the faith? Different authors would
give very different answers; and a follower of Averroes might have
very different ideas about what constituted 'consistency' from those
of the archbishop. William's own theories definitely rejected an
Aristotelian account of the theory of knowledge. The same is true
of the theories of Robert Grosseteste, an Englishman of the same
period (1170–1253), brought up in a native tradition of learning,
so far as we can make out, independent of the traditions of the Paris
schools. (Grosseteste, incidentally, has the distinction that later he
was regarded as a hero both by Protestants and by Catholics of
the Counter-Reformation, and he had the glory of being the first
scholar to make and use subject indexes of the books he had read.)
Another Englishman, Roger Bacon (c.1212–c.1292) – who had
a high regard for Grosseteste – rather tartly drew the attention of
Aristotelians to the fact that Aristotle himself argued against the
undue admission of faulty authorities – such as, no doubt, Aristotle
himself, on Bacon's view.

The Augustinian tradition was thus alive and kicking: but there
were limits to the amount of Aristotelian teaching that could be
absorbed in this way. Nor was there much hope for a workable
synthesis from the remarkable, not to say bizarre, theories of
Raymond Llull (c.1232–1315; both Christian name and surname
are given in a wide variety of spellings). He was an isolated thinker
from Majorca who proposed to synthesise all existing knowledge
and provide an infallible means of discovering new truths by the
identification and recombination of nine basic concepts. (He is now
chiefly famous for the elegant and ingenious system of concentric
circles he used to provide for possible recombinations.)

The problem was that while these attempts at a partial synthesis
were being made and were failing, the Aristotelians of the faculty of
Arts were continuing in their own way. We have no details of who
were the great figures in the development of a radical Aristotelianism
on Averroist lines in the earlier part of the thirteenth century: but
by 1270 this radical Aristotelianism was clearly a serious force in

the University, and it must have been growing up over the years. What could be done to avoid a complete separation between faith and reason, and thus the failure of Augustine's project?

7.2 A NEW SYNTHESIS

The first thing that was needed was to establish what Aristotle had actually said. Valuable insights of, for example, Avicenna, Averroes, and Maimonides, might be incorporated into this interpretation; but any commentary made by any of these on Aristotle which were inconsistent with the truths of the Christian faith could be left on one side without regret and without apology. It was going to be hard enough to deal with any difficulties or errors in the writings of Aristotle himself, without having to try to deal with the additional errors of later non-Christian and sometimes anti-Christian commentators as well. These commentators had authority, but it was fairly slight: when they agreed neither with the obvious sense of Aristotle nor with the Christian faith they could simply be ignored. The authority of Aristotle was a far more serious matter, and could not be treated so cavalierly; but for that very reason it was seen as good to ensure that the errors taught in Aristotle's name were cut down to a minimum. Two individuals in the thirteenth century stand out in their performance of this task, with a third standing as the triumphant heir of their achievement.

One great figure in the attempt to get at Aristotle himself, undistorted by Averroist interpretations, was less a philosopher than a translator. Philosophers and other scholars often look down on the humble task of the translator, but a good translation has more than once contributed greatly to philosophical understanding. William of Moerbeke (c.1215–1286) had spent time on Papal diplomatic missions to the Byzantine East, and had picked up enough Greek to be a good scholar of that language, in a period when few others in the West could boast of that distinction. Grosseteste is the only other distinguished figure of the period who occurs to me as a good Greek scholar. Moerbeke devoted his life as a scholar, after retiring from Papal administration, to producing new Latin translations directly from good Greek texts, to replace the former

Latin translations of Arabic translations of Syriac translations of God knows to what extent corrupt Greek originals. With these new translations, a scholar in the West could be fairly sure that whatever errors a text in front of him might contain, they would at least be Aristotle's own errors, and not those of some Muslim trying to fit Aristotle with his own beliefs. The translations are fairly literal, but good and clear: they are no more difficult to read than is Aristotle himself, for someone with good Greek. The contrast with the older translations is remarkable, as anyone with a smattering of Latin can ascertain.

The other, and perhaps greater, figure in this attempt to get at the original meaning of Aristotle was Albert of Cologne (1206–1280): St Albert the Great, as he is known. He explicitly regarded his task as that of interpreting Aristotle to the Latins: telling them exactly what Aristotle himself had said. Albert himself was well established in the Augustinian approach to learning, and contributed to its development, but he made no attempt at a synthesis of the two, perhaps deliberately. This was so much the case that the later school that called itself, with much justification, 'Albertist', was definitely Augustinian and neo-Platonist. In commenting on Aristotle, Albert was content to put forward what he understood as Aristotle's view in all its fullness, completely separately from his own very different views, leaving it to others to make what synthesis could be made.

Albert was fortunate enough to find a pupil of genius who he was able to inspire with this project. The highest point of the development of medieval thought in the West, by fairly widespread consent, is found in the work of St Thomas Aquinas (c.1125–1274). It is impossible to say of this author whether he was an Augustinian or an Aristotelian. We have already, in Chapter 2, drawn attention to the enormous bulk of his citations of the authority of Aristotle; a bulk matched only by that of his citations of Augustine. No other authority rivals these two, for Aquinas. Modern philosophers who read him, who are familiar with Aristotle and not with Augustine, see only the Aristotelianism. Among his contemporaries, though, attitudes were more nuanced. It was the old-fashioned Neoplatonic Augustinians who noticed (and disliked) his Aristotelianism. Meanwhile the more radical Aristotelians, or even Averroists, among his contemporaries – whose interpretation of Aristotle he strongly opposed – had no doubt that in their great debate with the Augustinians Aquinas was clearly on the opposite side.

For Aquinas, the synthesis was to be achieved not through the victory of one tendency or approach over the other, whether achieved by the imposition of legal authority or by some more covert method. Such a method might be that which the Augustinians of the earlier part of the century had attempted, of piecemeal interpretation which made Aristotle fit their own system but deprived him of originality and vigour. Or it might be what the radical Arisotelian of his day had attempted – slowly building up an unassailable popular position in the faculty of Arts. For Aquinas, each question was to be listened to in an open manner, and concepts that derived from either approach were to be used when suitable. In the use and the relating of such concepts a new system of concepts could be built up, which would be internally consistent, and would be capable of meeting objections brought forward from either side.

Crucial here was the use of the notion of analogy. This notion was used in a programmatic way by Aquinas in his early discussion of the concept of truth. For the Aristotelians, truth was something that arose in the match of the human mind with the world. For the traditional Augustinians, on the other hand 'truth' was another name for God. Aquinas, in his early and brilliant 'disputed question' *On Truth* (a collection of closely related *questions*, in the technical sense) managed to reconcile these two answers, showing how they could both be systematically related, as analogical concepts. The truth which is God is primary and fundamental in the order of reality, of existence; but in our usage of the word 'truth' the Aristotelian sense, in fact, comes first. Aquinas achieved all this by expanding the Aristotelian notion of truth as match between mind and reality to include all minds, giving precedence to God's; and by observing that the direction of match can go either way. It may be a question of the mind's having to match with reality, as when we observe and describe the world; or it may be a case of reality's having to match with the mind, as in the case of our productions and actions, or in the case of the world's relationship to God's creative mind.

The method by which such syntheses can be made is perhaps best seen if we return to the question examined in Chapter 4, in the discussion of the difficulties involved in the Augustinian approach. We asked there, 'How are we to reject the false teachings of the philosophers?', and saw that to rely on the faith itself in carrying out this task might lead to fideism, and thus to a real failure to reconcile faith and reason,

Aquinas's answer to this is very clear. We know that the false teachings of the philosophers are in fact false because we have the understanding that follows on from faith. But the fact that these teachings are against faith is not the only reason why those answers are false. If Plato or Aristotle said something false, then they must have made a mistake somewhere, and if we are only clever enough we will be able to find it out. As Aquinas says in the article of the *Summa Theologiae* cited in Chapter 2 on the question of authority (I, q.1, a.8): 'Arguments which go against the faith are not proofs but refutable fallacies'.

Aquinas thought, then, that with a suitable development of some concepts – for example, that of analogy – there might be sufficient resources within Aristotle's own system to refute the mistakes that occurred within that system. It was easier for an Aristotelian like Aquinas to avoid the mistakes Aristotle had made because since his time Aristotle's own invention of logic had been refined by its development in the medieval tradition. But it was also easier because, as Augustine would have maintained, someone like Aquinas also had the understanding that faith gives. We can say, then, that Aquinas's aim was the Augustinian one of refuting Aristotle's errors by incorporating into Aquinas's own understanding the truths at which Aristotle himself had arrived.

Thus, for all Aquinas's Aristotelianism, for him to have achieved his aim would be a triumph, in a sense, of the Augustinian approach; and this, even though it would necessarily involve abandoning many of the Neoplatonist theories that Augustine had found valuable in the development of his own understanding. We might represent Aquinas as trying to do what Augustine himself would have done, if he had had the teachings of Aristotle as easily available to him as those of the Neoplatonists. If Aquinas achieved his aim, Augustinianism would not have been defeated but would have triumphed. The only defeat would be for those Neoplatonist and conservative Augustinians who could not distinguish between what was essential and what was accidental in Augustine's own teaching and project. The understanding based on faith would once again have triumphed over error, and it would have incorporated, as Augustine wished it to incorporate, all human wisdom.

But what of the other difficulties that were felt about Aristotle? What about the fact that his system seemed to provide a complete explanation of the world without any need for divine intervention? The answers Aquinas gave to questions such as these were perhaps the high point of his achievement. Again and again he was able to show that while Aristotle provided a complete explanation of the system of the world, that very system as a whole looks beyond itself. It is true that in Aquinas we lose, for example, the claim that the everyday occurrence of human knowledge needs God's direct intervention, a claim that was very dear to Augustine. But according to Aquinas the existence of the world and of the mind, of truth and knowledge, as well-matched and systematic wholes that function and relate to one another independently of God's special intervention, itself points beyond the world, beyond the finite mind, beyond finite truth, to God.

The notion of analogy thus comes up again. Aquinas thought he could show that, like the word 'true', the words 'good', 'existent', and the like, have, as Aristotle saw, a perfectly valid application within the world. But he also thought that to understand these uses fully we have to understand that they are analogous. The primary use of such words is as names for God: without God, the good and the true could not exist and could not therefore be either known or talked about.

In a similar way, Aquinas claimed that he could show that the Aristotelian concepts of purpose (or point), function and fulfilment, when applied to human beings, pointed beyond themselves, and indeed beyond the created world as a whole. He believes that the characteristic rational activities, or function, of human beings, are, on Aristotle's own showing, incapable of being fully realised in this life. Humans, therefore, cannot fully achieve their point – what they are for. If they are to do so, it must be by God's gift. Augustine had said that God had made us for himself, and our hearts are restless until they rest in him. Aquinas thinks that Aristotle himself might have realised this, if he had, like Augustine and Aquinas himself, the understanding that is based on faith.

Many who start to read medieval philosophy or theology start by reading Aquinas. This is quite natural: he is an excellent author, and does in some way represent the high point of development of these studies in the period. If readers then go on to look at other authors they may sometimes feel disappointed. But there is a problem with reading only Aquinas; and it is that in his work there seems to be no problem. The synthesis he achieved seems effortless. As a result, it is very hard to realise why it seemed so problematic to his contemporaries. Even harder to understand why his synthesis was never generally accepted. Only for a period in the sixteenth century, and even then only in some circles, did Aquinas achieve anything like widespread recognition. But it petered out until the nineteenth century. In a similar way, if one reads Dante – himself a figure of intellectual synthesis and reconciliation like Aquinas, whom he greatly admired and often followed – the medieval world-picture as a whole seems completely harmonious and extremely valuable. It is hard to realise the difficulties that contemporaries found in the systems of thought represented by those two almost perfect works, the *Summa Theologiae* and the *Divine Comedy*.

The likely reason why the synthesis of Aquinas was not in fact accepted by his contemporaries was that the two sides in the debate had already grown too far apart. To the conservative Augustinians Aquinas appeared an out-and-out Aristotelian, while to the Aristotelians he appeared a traitor, as one without the courage of his convictions, a temporiser. There was, it is true, agreement in accepting some parts of his achievement: the second part of the Part Two of the *Summa Theologiae*, for example, which deals with the virtues, was widely accepted and widely read. But this was because it was possible – and still is – to take this section of the work and slot it into a quite different framework, a framework that was basically Aristotelian or basically conservative, Augustinian and Neoplatonist. The right framework, the framework that Aquinas himself had crafted, in which this section found its proper place and proper relation with the rest of philosophy and theology, was ignored.

It is true that the radical Aristotelianism or 'Latin Averroism' of Aquinas's day, represented by Siger of Brabant (1235–1282) was rebuked by a series of authoritative pronouncements in 1270. More to the point, Aquinas's arguments against the radicals' positions – particularly their view that there was only one active intellect for the whole human race, or the view attributed to them that inconsistencies between faith and reason could be cleared up by distinguishing two kinds of truth – seem to have been effective. We do not find these views appearing again in anything like the same form. This victory over radical Aristotelianism was surely achieved as much by Aquinas's arguments as by the decrees of the Archbishop of Paris, which had never succeeded before.

But it would be easy for conservative Augustinians to represent Aquinas' own views on the analogical nature of the concept of truth as falling under the Archbishop's strictures. Indeed, we find certain other propositions which Aquinas definitely upheld being condemned in a large rag-bag of allegedly unorthodox theses in 1277. Aquinas's synthesis, then, must be held to have failed: not failed as a theoretical synthesis, but certainly to have failed to find acceptance as a reconciliation of different schools, approaches and tendencies of thought.

7.3 THE CLAIM OF AUTONOMY

The synthesis was rejected, as satisfying neither side: it could, perhaps, satisfy only someone like Aquinas who was capable of sharing in the attitudes of both approaches. Aquinas' contemporary and colleague (and indeed friend) in Paris, St Bonaventure (1221–1274) held that Aristotle was only of interest as a natural philosopher, a philosopher who could explain about the bodies in the world that we can see. Bonaventure would not admit Aristotle as a metaphysician, that is, as a valuable guide to the nature of knowledge, of human fulfilment, or the existence and nature of God.

Among others the cry went up for autonomy between faith

and reason, between theology and philosophy. It seems as if the first weighty claim for autonomy was made in the name of theology, by John Duns Scotus (c.1265–1308). This theologian from Berwickshire refused to admit the synthesis which Aquinas had made.

Scotus rejected both the conservative theory of knowledge, which relied on divine illumination, and Aquinas's Aristotelian theory, according to which the mind matched up to reality by receiving the forms of things. Scotus insisted that human beings had a direct intellectual knowledge or 'intuition' of individual things in the world, a theory which was to be later in part developed and in part contradicted by William of Ockham, the great logician of the following generation. The important point of Scotus's metaphysics was the individualness of each existent.

Scotus also rejected Aquinas's account of analogy, which he regarded as being close to denying that there can be any accurate knowledge at all. 'Existence', for Scotus, is a term with a single, univocal meaning. Interestingly, he combined this claim – which would be supported by many contemporaries of ours – with a new understanding of the notions of possibility and necessity, an understanding which again has a strong likeness to the contemporary explanation of these notions in terms of what happens in some or in all 'possible worlds'. It is often commented, and worth commenting, that such a view in fact destroys what is especially significant or interesting in these notions. Instead of a basic conception of what might happen, as contrasted with what does in fact happen, we make what might happen equivalent to what does in fact happen, not here but elsewhere, in some other possible world. By Scotus's work, then, the distinctively Aristotelian concepts of form, analogy, necessity and possibility are all undermined.

The synthesis created by Aquinas was unacceptable to Scotus in many ways. To his eyes, it did not leave enough room for God's freedom and God's action in the world. Aquinas, Scotus thought, had based his synthesis on the natural intelligibility of the world, on the grounds that the world was the work of the divine mind, and thus intelligible. But, said Scotus, the world was also a work of God's will and God's power; by insisting on the rational ordering of the world, Aquinas was taking away from God His power and freedom to have made the world differently. The followers of Scotus could perhaps accept the second part of the Part Two of Aquinas's *Summa Theologiae*, if they wished, as a good description of the way things actually are in the world, of the way in which God has, as a matter of fact, willed human flourishing to be brought about. But, they thought, God could have willed to bring about human flourishing in some other, quite different way. There was, for the Scotists, no kind of natural necessity about human virtues, as Aristotle and Aquinas had thought. Moreover, they thought that in Aristotle there was no room, and in Aquinas insufficient room, for the concept of moral obligation. The autonomy of theology – in the shape of reflections on the ten commandments or otherwise – had to be ensured. Aquinas, for Scotus and his followers, had tried to prove too much by means of reason alone. More must be left for the work of faith.

Naturally enough, this claim for autonomy in the name of theology provoked a reaction among the philosophers, the Aristotelians of the Arts faculties. Perhaps the Latin Averroists had never really held that there were two truths – and, indeed, it is very hard to pin down a text where any of them make this claim. Perhaps this was only the logical conclusion from some of the doctrines they did hold, put into their mouths by opponents such as Aquinas. In any case, by this time that school seemed to have been defeated. But as time went on, and the theologians proclaimed their autonomy, there came to be more and more a demand for autonomy from the philosophers too. It is a very bad sign, surely, when we find the English logician William of Ockham (c.1285–1349) stating what he claims is a logical law, and then blandly admitting that this or that proposition of Christian faith is a counter-example to that law. If a law is a logical law, then surely there should be no counter-examples or exceptions. If the logical law is true, then either the proposition of faith which apparently contradicts it is false, or it has been misunderstood. Or, on the other hand, if the proposition of faith is unequivocal and true, then the alleged logical law can be no law at all. It is surely not permissible to put down side by side the two statements – the alleged logical law and the apparently contradictory proposition of the faith –

and do nothing to reconcile them: yet this is what Ockham rather frequently does.

Personally, Ockham and those like him may have believed in the truth of the doctrine of the Church: but if they did they had also to believe that the human mind was not adequate to reach the truth about logic on its own. If they held that the human mind – in particular, their own minds – was adequate to this task, then they would be accusing the Church of teaching falsehood, and would thus be falling into heresy. The demand for autonomy of faith from reason, or of reason from faith, from whichever side it was made, always had the same effect: that of destroying any possibility of synthesis, and thus of destroying any possibility of achieving the aim of the medieval intellectual project.

7.4 DEGENERATION

This destruction took a very long time. Indeed, what is really surprising is how long the medieval tradition of intellectual inquiry was able to continue after the claim for autonomy had made itself heard. Aquinas died in 1274: it is not until Descartes that the modern age in philosophy begins. And during those three hundred years there was a great deal of work done that seems of immense interest even, or perhaps especially, to contemporary philosophers.

There were two things that happened in philosophy in the centuries following the failure of Aquinas's synthesis to gain acceptance. One is that the tradition became fragmented. As a result, not only was theology separated from philosophy, to the detriment of both, but logic was separated from metaphysics and the theory of knowledge, metaphysics was separated from ethics, ethics was separated from political theory. Above all, there appeared a number of partial traditions, schools which traced their origins to some great thinker, often of the thirteenth or early fourteenth century – Albert, Aquinas, Llull, Scotus, for example – and which developed their master's thought. Valuable work was done, but no matter how valuable, it was almost by definition unacceptable to those of different partial traditions or schools. Scholars became incapable of assimilating truths and insights found in other schools.

The second feature of the later fourteenth and fifteenth centuries, which also helps to make the work done in this period more familiar to contemporary philosophers was the following. During this period philosophy could to a great extent be defined, as it can today, in terms of the problems that it dealt with. The earlier medieval ideal demanded that there should be slow but steady progress. A problem would be presented, debated and re-debated, and eventually solved to the satisfaction of the philosophical world as a whole – and the theological world, too. And then there would be a move on to the discussion of a new problem, perhaps a problem that had been revealed in the debates leading up to the solution of the earlier one. In this way the ideal of earlier medieval philosophy was like the ideal of modern science. But in the later period it is possible to see author after author discussing and presenting radically new or different solutions to the same apparently insoluble or intractable problems. And that is what happens in philosophy today.

Perhaps, both then and now, philosophers hope that one of them will throw up a solution that will compel the assent of everyone, and then progress can be made to another problem: but all the historical evidence seems to show that such a hope is vain. There is a theoretical reason, too, why this should be so: there can be no solution that compels assent from the different schools and partial traditions when they all have such very different starting points. It is not just that contemporary philosophers, or the philosophers of the later Middle Ages, do not agree on when a problem has been solved; often they or we do not agree on what it is for a problem to be solved, or whether there is a problem at all. It is therefore very significant that we find, for example, both Scotus and Ockham attacking earlier thinkers on the grounds that what they had taken to be proven was not proven at all.

William of Ockham is, in fact, a figure of great importance here. He was primarily a logician, and a logician of great ingenuity. He took over the logical doctrine of nominalism – that words signify only individuals, not forms or natures – and refined it of some of the crudity of earlier nominalists. He then applied the insights provided by his own powerful logical work, and that of his predecessors, in other fields. In this way he challenged the already existing schools and partial traditions – which his followers called the *'via antiqua'* 'old way' – in the name of his own radical solutions, the *'via moderna'* or 'modern way'.

If words signify only individuals, then our minds, whose knowledge is expressed by words, can know only individuals. By the principle known as 'Ockham's razor' – the principle that we should not postulate the existence of an entity unless we have sufficient reason for doing so – Ockham concluded that only individuals exist. (It is worth mentioning that while the use of this principle as a principle of methodology may not go farther back than Ockham, Aquinas, for example, clearly accepts a yet stronger metaphysical version of the same principle; what can be explained by fewer principles should not be explained by more.) By his use of the principle, Ockham came to reject, for example, the interpretation Aquinas gave to Aristotle's theory of knowledge, that our minds are aware of things through the presence in the mind, in a non-material, non-individual mode, of the very same forms that exist in things. In consequence, Ockham thought that there is no need to suppose that forms or natures exist at all outside the mind: the kinds to which substances belong became, for Ockham, mere classifications imposed on reality by the mind.

On the basis of his new, more radical standpoint, Ockham was able, perhaps, to achieve some limited synthesis within philosophy: but only at very great cost. Like Scotus, he claimed that many of the alleged demonstrations of earlier philosophers and thinkers were not proofs at all. An enormous amount remained theoretically unprovable for Ockham, even, for example, the existence of human free will. He also found no possibility of real purpose, point, or finality in non-animate things, thus destroying a key feature of Aristotle's theory of scientific explanation. Ockham went far beyond Scotus in moral questions, and insisted on God's freedom to the extent that he was willing to claim that it was possible for God to command a man to hate God, and that to hate God would then, for that man, be the right thing to do. If we can be confident that this will not happen, it is only because of a trust in God's goodness: God wouldn't want to confuse us so much.

It should come as no surprise, then, that at least one of

Ockham's followers, Nicholas of Autrecourt (c.1300 to ?after 1350) came to deny even what remained of Aristotle's theory of explanation and causality. He denied even the reality of substance and of efficient causal connections, using arguments similar to those which eighteenth-century empiricists such as the Scottish philosopher David Hume were to use much later.

What is surprising is that another logician in the Ockhamist tradition, John Buridan (died c.1360) should have nevertheless managed to use Aristotelian concepts of explanation to refine Aristotle's own physics and astronomy. Buridan developed a theory of motion that had come down to him from the early sixth-century Greek Aristotelian, John Philoponus, and came to the conclusion that the physical laws that applied on earth could equally well apply in the heavens – a conclusion that Aristotle himself had strongly denied. As a result Buridan came near to formulating a principle that can be seen as roughly equivalent to Newton's second law of motion.

A similar figure was that of Nicholas Oresme (?1323–1382) whose work on acceleration came down, through Leonardo da Vinci, to Galileo. He can thus be considered, like Buridan, as one of the fathers of modern science. What is curious about these people is the way in which they managed to escape the influence of Ockhamist and Scotist attacks on Aristotelian concepts of explanation, and to make their explanatory developments within physics and astronomy. It is sometimes said that Buridan and Oresme were only able to make such progress precisely because of the work that Ockham and others had done to overthrow old prejudices. This claim is absolutely ridiculous, but perhaps it is not surprising. It is just another demonstration of the strange things that modern people say about the Middle Ages, simply because they themselves have no grasp of the importance of the Aristotelian theory of explanation for the development of modern science.

Ockham had many followers: Ockhamist nominalism became the dominant school in logic. But in philosophy as a whole Ockhamism became just one more of the rival fragments of tradition. This confused and confusing situation provoked reactions, even before the final and crushing reactions of Luther and Descartes. We find, for example, in the works of Meister Eckhart (c.1260–1327) and other later authors a rejection of all rational ways to get to God through a knowledge of the world. For Eckhart, the only use for philosophical concepts was to help clarify both the knowledge of God that was given in mystical experience, and the nature of that experience itself. Not surprisingly, perhaps, his efforts in this line turned out to be rather unorthodox: his only defence against charges of heresy was that his language had to be understood metaphorically. This may be a sound defence, but it is no way to achieve a synthesis. But what else could he do? Once the concept of analogy had been lost or demoted, there seemed to be no room in language for anything other than literal expression or metaphor.

A similar rejection of the work of his contemporaries marks the writings of Nicholas of Cusa (1401–1464). He attempted a new synthesis: but it was a synthesis based on the idea of synthesis itself. All opposites, for Nicholas, were reconciled in God. (This kind of notion is sometimes called the 'With one mighty bound, Jack was free' school of philosophy: solving difficulties by ignoring them.) Nicholas's mighty bound failed to endear itself to the opposed rival schools; it thus turned out to be just another failed attempt to answer the basic and by this time perennial questions about what could be considered to constitute a reasonable explanation.

A striking aspect of the fragmentation of tradition is shown by developments in political philosophy, in which Ockham himself took a hand. A great practical problem for political thinkers in the Middle Ages was the frequently renewed conflict between the authority of the Holy Roman Emperor and the authority of the Pope. (And when the King of France took a hand, as he often did, matters became even more complicated, practically if not always theoretically.) Aquinas, like others, had attempted a reconciliation and synthesis of rival claims in this matter, claiming divine authority for all just rulers, but restricting the essential power of the Pope to spiritual matters, in which the Emperor should not interfere. As the tradition fragmented, this solution ceased to be acceptable: admirable in theory, it left room for a whole fringe of borderline disputes which this theory on its own could not resolve. Political writers came to attend only to the notions employed within their own Papalist or Imperialist traditions, and genuine debate ceased. It was succeeded by the ever more strident repetition of rival claims, quite often backed up in practice by force. (Since the Pope's military force was negligible, this is where the King of France used to come in.) Some claimed that the Pope had authority over the Emperor, even in (at least some) secular matters, others that the Emperor had authority over the Pope, even in (at least some) spiritual matters. The Imperialists even intervened in debates about the nature of authority within the Church, favouring the view that a Church Council, perhaps called by the Emperor against the Pope's will, had full authority over the Pope. It was not, in fact, until interest in Aquinas was renewed, in some parts of Italy and in Spain during the second half of the sixteenth century, that his doctrine came to be widely accepted as at least setting out the limits of possible debate. By this time, of course, problems between the Pope and secular rulers had taken on quite a different colour, since some rulers had turned Protestant and refused to recognise any authority for the Pope at all, not even a limited one: as Bishop of Rome or Prince of the Papal States.

The last stage in the separation of political theory from theology and even from ethics was achieved, notoriously, by Niccolò Machiavelli (1469–1527). We normally think of him as a Renaissance man, one who comes after the break with the Middle Ages: historians of ideas, indeed, even speak quite often of his predecessor Marsilius of Padua (died c.1342) as a post-medieval thinker. But if we are to speak of the history of philosophy, we need make our historical break on philosophical grounds. It should thus come later, with the foundationalism of Descartes; or, if we are to speak of what is sometimes called 'Renaissance philosophy', its marks are an obsession with Plato and with the human soul, neither of which are to be found in either Marsilius or Machiavelli. Or, thematically, we might prefer to put the break earlier, when Scotus or Ockham proclaimed and enforced autonomy and undid the possibility of the medieval project. Either way, in so far as Machiavelli is a philosopher, he is a medieval philosopher, part of a very definite trend within medieval philosophy: the heir of a degenerate, fragmented medieval tradition.

Even the genuine achievements of the later Middle Ages – in logic, say – eventually ceased. The real achievements of medieval logic seem to have been abandoned in the early sixteenth century, in most of Europe, as futile complications that added nothing to what the hearer could understand of the speaker's meaning, or the reader could understand of the writer's meaning. The question of communication had become paramount: in so far as there is a real difference between medieval and Renaissance thought, this point is part of it. It did not help that medieval logical texts were written in an extremely stylised technical language, which appeared gross and ridiculous to people who were beginning to value good Latin style above almost anything else.

There was a late flowering of logic in Paris in the early and mid-sixteenth century, brought about by a group of Scotsmen and Spaniards under the inspiration of the logician and historian John Mair: but they had few or no followers outside Spain and the Spanish dominions. One nice detail of the history of logic is that the last good solid textbook of medieval logic, read by Descartes, among others, was written and printed in Mexico. But by the time of Descartes logic had ceased to be of importance, and, until the nineteenth century, had even ceased to be taught in any intelligent form (though in an unintelligent and indeed nonsensical form it continued to be part of school or university curricula). Theology was becoming of more crucial importance in the sixteenth century – in its name people were being burnt or disembowelled, sometimes, as in England, both – but the shift towards theology does not seem to be a sufficient explanation of why suddenly, everywhere except Spain and Mexico, the great medieval tradition of logic should have foundered.

Perhaps the only acceptable explanation is some version of this one, which is usually given: that the best minds of the period were distracted by the great religious (and political, social, economic and military) upheavals that followed on from Luther. However, one might also argue that the abandonment of logic is rather another symptom of the rejection of tradition that Luther himself exemplifies. It is the rejection of tradition as a whole that needs explaining, not this or that particular feature or consequence of it. Perhaps the explanation is quite simple. The fragmented and rival traditions that survived down to that day were bulky and contradictory, and, above all, they could not all be embraced or even understood by one person. Even though from the outside they might all look equally valid to take up the study of one meant rejecting the authority of all the others. To accept the basic concepts and principles of one meant to reject as false and often as meaningless, the basic concepts and principles of the others. This, perhaps, is why in the end Descartes came to reject all systems that were held on the basis of tradition. By Descartes' time, it seemed there could be no possible rational ground for holding to one tradition rather than to another. It was no longer the case, as once it had been, that there was a single tradition which could be appealed to. It was not possible to demand willingness to accept the authority of a single tradition as the condition for being admitted to rational debate. Rational debate between the rival fragments of the tradition had long before ceased. It begins to look as if we should ask not why Descartes reacted in the way that he did, but how on earth the situation of fragmented medieval tradition had been able to endure for so long without provoking a reaction such as Descartes'. Perhaps the answer is that only a genius like Descartes (and one has to regard him as a genius, even if he was mistaken: someone who can give a wrong turn to philosophy for three hundred years must be a genius) could have reacted sufficiently solidly and influentially.

The story, then, has brought us to the Cartesian reaction, to the start of the increasingly desperate search for self-evident first principles. We know that this very soon gave rise to the suggestion of all kinds of rival candidates for the status of foundational principles, and that, as a matter of history, the Cartesian project has failed. We are nowadays in as bad a situation in philosophy as they were in the sixteenth century. Perhaps the only hope is for a return to the acceptance of some kind of authority, and to begin again from there. But, alas, the suggestion is highly unwelcome to nearly all contemporary philosophers; and even if it were welcome, which authority would we choose?

Chronological List
of Important Figures

Plato (c.428–c.348 BC)
Aristotle (384–322 BC)
Plotinus (c.204–270)
Porphyry (c.232–c.304)
St Augustine (354–430)
Chalcidius (late 4th to early 5th centuries)
Boethius (c.480–524)
John Philoponus (early 6th century)
Pseudo-Dionysius the Areopagite (6th century)
St John Damascene (c.676–c.754)
John Scotus Eriugena (c.810–c.875)
Avicenna (Ibn Sina, 980–1036)
St Anselm (1033–1109)
Hugo of St Victor (died 1141)
Roscelin (c.1050–1120)
Abelard (1079–1142)
St Bernard (1090–1153)
Averroes (Ibn Rushd 1126–1198)
Maimonides (Moishe ben Maimon, 1135–1204)
William of Auvergne (d. 1249)
Robert Grosseteste (c.1170–1253)
St Albert the Great (1206–1280)

Roger Bacon (c.1212–c.1292)
William of Moerbeke (c.1215–1286)
St Bonaventure (1221–1274)
St Thomas Aquinas (1224–1274)
Raymond Llull (c.1232–1315)
Siger of Brabant (1235–1282)
Meister Eckhart (c.1260–1327)
John Duns Scotus (c.1265–1308)
Marsilius of Padua (died c.1342)
William of Ockham (c.1285–1349)
Nicholas of Autrecourt (c.1300–?after 1350)
John Buridan (died c.1360)
Nicholas Oresme (?1323–1382)
Nicholas of Cusa (1401–1464)
Niccolò Machiavelli (1469–1527)
René Descartes (1596–1650)

Bibliography

Anscombe, G.E.M. and P.T. Geach, *Three Philosophers*, Blackwell 1961.

Anselm, Saint, *The Prayers and Meditations of St Anselm,* trans. B. Ward, Penguin 1973.

Aquinas, Saint Thomas, *Summa Theologiae*, ed. T. Gilby, Eyre and Spottiswoode 1963–75.

Aquinas, Saint Thomas, *The Philosophy of Thomas Aquinas: Introductory Readings*, ed. C.F.J. Martin, Routledge 1988.

Augustine, Saint, *Confessions*, trans. H. Chadwick, Oxford University Press 1991.

Barnes, J., *Aristotle*, Oxford University Press 1982.

Boethius, *The Consolation of Philosophy*, trans. V.E. Watts, Penguin 1976.

Broadie, A., *Introduction to Medieval Logic* (2nd edn), Oxford University Press 1993.

Chadwick, H., *Augustine*, Oxford University Press 1986.

Copleston, F.A., *History of Philosophy* Vol. 2, Westminster, Maryland: Newman bookshop 1946–75.

Copleston, F.A., *History of Medieval Philosophy*, Methuen 1972.

Copleston, F.A., *Aquinas*, Search Press 1976.

Duns Scotus, Blessed John, *Philosophical Writings*, a selection edited and translated by A. Wolter, Nelson 1962.

Gibson, M.M.T., *Boethius*, Blackwell 1981.

Gilson, E., *The Christian Philosophy of St Augustine*, trans. L.E.M. Lynch, Gollancz 1961.

Kenny, A.J.P., *Aquinas*, Oxford University Press 1980.

Kenny, A.J.P., *Aquinas on Mind*, Routledge 1993.

Kirwan, C., *Augustine*, Routledge 1989.

Knowles, D., *The Evolution of Medieval Thought* (2nd edn), Longman 1988.

Kretzmann, N., A.J.P. Kenny and J. Pinborg, *Cambridge History of Later Medieval Philosophy*, Cambridge University Press 1982.

Leff, G., *William of Ockham: The Metamorphosis of Scholastic Discourse*, Manchester University Press 1975.

Macintyre, A., *Whose Justice? Which Nationality?*, Duckworth 1988.

Macintyre, A., *Three Rival Versions of Moral Enquiry*, Duckworth 1990.

Marenbon, J., *Early Medieval Philosophy (480–1150): An Introduction*, Routledge and Kegan Paul 1983.

Marenbon, J., *Later Medieval Philosophy (1150–1350): An Introduction*, Routledge and Kegan Paul 1987.

Ockham, William of, *Philosophical Writings*, a selection ed. and trans. P. Boehner, Bobbs-Merrill 1964.

FURTHER READING

Some understanding of Aristotle would be valuable: see Barnes (1982), or the more difficult essay 'Aristotle' in Anscombe and Geach (1961). Good general introductions are Copleston (1946–75 and 1972), Knowles (1988) and Marenbon (1983 and 1987). Important and fairly accessible texts are the *Confessions* of Augustine (1991), *The Consolation of Philosophy* of Boethius (1976), and the *Monologion* and *Proslogion* of Anselm (1973). For the more systematic later period it may be worth reading Kretzmann et al. (1982). For an introduction to Aquinas, read 'Aquinas' in Anscombe and Geach (1961), Copleston (1976), or Kenny (1980). A good transition to reading the text of Aquinas may be provided by *The Philosophy of Thomas Aquinas* (1988) or Kenny (1993). Leff (1975) will give a good introduction to Ockham. On Scotus, see A. Broadie, *The Shadow of Scotus* (Edinburgh: T. & T. Clark, 1995).

Index

Note: References to individual authorities also cover their thought, e.g. 'Aristotle' subsumes 'Aristotelianism'.

141